Success. guides

Leckie ✕ Leckie

Intermediate 2
Hospitality

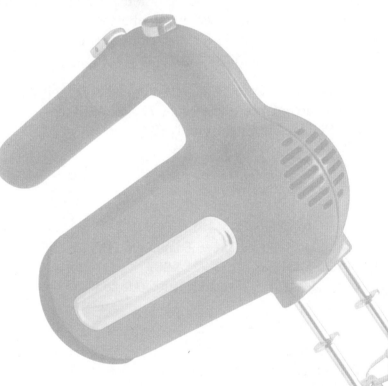

Edna Hepburn ✕ Jean McAllister

Text © 2008 Edna Hepburn and Jean McAllister
Design and layout © 2008 Leckie & Leckie
Cover image © Caleb Rutherford

01/301008

ISBN 978-1-84372-497-1

Published by
Leckie & Leckie Ltd, 3rd floor, 4 Queen Street, Edinburgh, EH2 1JE
Tel: 0131 220 6831 Fax: 0131 225 9987
enquiries@leckieandleckie.co.uk   www.leckieandleckie.co.uk

Special thanks to
Caleb Rutherford (cover design),
The Partnership Publishing Solutions (creative packaging),
Eduardo Iturralde (illustration),
Thora Barron (content review),
Roda Morrison (copy-edit),
Tara Watson (proofread),
Dr Laurence Errington (index).

A CIP Catalogue record for this book is available from the British Library.

Leckie & Leckie Ltd is a division of Huveaux plc.

Contents

Introduction

How to use this Success Guide   4

Practical Cookery Skills for the Hospitality Industry 1

Kitchen organisation   6
Hygiene   7
Safety   9
Storage of foods   10
Weighing and measuring   11

Practical Cookery Skills for the Hospitality Industry 2

What's this unit all about?   12
Food preparation techniques and equipment   13
Culinary terms   27
Presentation techniques   28
Assessment practice   35

Food Preparation for Healthy Eating

What's this unit all about?   36
Ingredients for healthy eating   37
Preparation techniques for healthy eating   44
Cookery methods for healthy eating   46
Planning your work   50
Costing of ingredients   54
Assessment practice   56

Foods of the World

What's this unit all about?   58
Introduction to India   60
1. Range of Indian traditional foods   61
2. Characteristics of traditional foodstuffs   62
3. Traditional dishes of India   68
4. Characteristics of traditional dishes   69
Introduction to Italy   73
1. Range of Italian traditional foods   74
2. Characteristics of traditional foodstuffs   75
3. Traditional dishes of Italy   81
4. Characteristics of traditional dishes   82
Assessment practice   86
How to do well in your practical assignment   87

How to do well in your practical assignment

Assessment practice answers   92

How to use this Success Guide

The information in this book should help you make good progress through the Intermediate 2 Hospitality: Practical Cookery course and so help you achieve the best possible grades.

Food Safety and Hygiene play an important part in all your practical activities so there is a separate area on this topic, but remember that this topic will also be covered in some way in each unit and will be assessed in the course assessment.

The chapters of this book are arranged to cover the course content of the three units in the Intermediate 2 course.

At the start of each chapter is a section called '**What's this unit all about?**' These pages will give you information on:

- the outcomes (what you have to do) for each unit
- the assessments for each unit
- what you have to know or do to pass each assessment.

At the end of each unit you will find **assessment practice.** These pages will give you an opportunity to practise the types of activity you will find in your National Assessment Bank items (NABs), issued by Scottish Qualifications Authority (SQA). You will have to pass the National Assessment Bank items, so it is a good idea to have some practice first. **Answers** for the assessment practice are found on pages 94–95.

What's in this book?

In this *Success Guide* the units are covered in the following order:

Practical Cookery Skills for the Hospitality Industry

The first two chapters will give you information about the food preparation skills, techniques and equipment you will use when preparing a wide range of dishes.

Food Preparation for Healthy Eating

This chapter will help you develop knowledge and skills to select ingredients and methods of preparing and cooking foods with the purpose of producing a range of dishes which will promote healthier eating.

Foods of the World

This chapter will give you some examples of traditional foodstuffs and dishes of two selected countries (Italy and India). This information can be used as guidance when you are compiling the report for your chosen country.

Course assessment

The course assessment is based on a practical assignment undertaken under controlled conditions. The course assessment is set by the SQA and will involve the planning and preparation of three different dishes, each with four portions, within 2½ hours. The dishes will be a starter, main course and a dessert. The assignment will include:

- at least one healthy dish
- at least one international dish
- a range of food preparation techniques, cookery processes and presentation techniques you have practised during the three units.

Useful information which will help you do well in your **practical assignment** is found on pages 88–93.

Other features of the book

Top Tips

Top Tips to help you be successful are included on each double page. These tips will:

- link to the course content
- give you tips for your practical work
- give you examination tips.

Quick Tests

These are short questions which will test your knowledge. Answers are also given but remember – don't cheat and look at them before you write your answers!

Leckie and Leckie Learning Lab

When you see this, it means that the activity or information is listed on the Leckie and Leckie Learning Lab. To find these, go to: www.leckieandleckie.co.uk, click on the Learning Lab button and navigate to the *Intermediate 2 Hospitality Success Guide* page.

Before starting this unit it is important to be aware of the following procedures in the hospitality industry.

- Kitchen organisation
- Personal hygiene
- Kitchen hygiene
- Safety
- Storage of foods
- Weighing and measuring

Kitchen organisation

Although you will not be examined on how a commercial kitchen is organised, it is important to have a little background knowledge of the organisation and roles of different individuals in the hospitality industry.

To become competent, skilled and employable in the hospitality industry the professional chef must work:→

A well-run kitchen will prepare and cook the correct amount of high-quality food for the required number of people, on time, with best use of staff, ingredients and equipment.

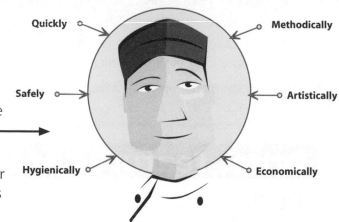

Quickly • Methodically • Safely • Artistically • Hygienically • Economically

The partie system

Some kitchens, particularly in large hotels and restaurants, use a system called the 'partie system' to organise roles and responsibilities in a professional environment. This involves the staff being divided into sections to carry out specific tasks, whether preparing or cooking the variety of foods. Other smaller establishments have adopted their own similar systems to suit their own kitchen staff and less complex menus. The chart below shows how a kitchen may be organised using the partie system.

Here are the main tasks of the following personnel:

Head chef is in overall charge of the kitchen. This includes allocating the work between the different kitchen sections and ensuring the results are of a standard that will contribute to the good reputation of their establishment.

Sous chef is an assistant to the Head chef and supervises all the work in the kitchen, as they have expert knowledge of all sections of the kitchen.

Chef de partie is in charge of a section of the work in the kitchen. This is the job of a specialist, e.g. they could be in charge of soups or pastries or fish dishes.

Commis chef is an assistant cook to the Chef de partie. There can be a number of Commis chefs in each section, depending on the amount of work to be done.

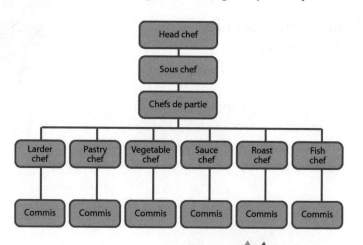

Head chef → Sous chef → Chefs de partie → Larder chef, Pastry chef, Vegetable chef, Sauce chef, Roast chef, Fish chef → Commis, Commis, Commis, Commis, Commis, Commis

Top Tip
When learning a skill, speed is not the most important thing to learn first – this will come with practice. It is essential that accuracy of procedure and improving performance comes first.

Hygiene

The most important requirement in the food industry is to ensure that the food which is prepared is **safe to eat.**

When we eat in restaurants we rely very much on good **personal** and **kitchen hygiene** from all food handlers involved in the food chain.

Personal hygiene

Good personal hygiene helps prevent food contamination by **people**; therefore the following points must be put into practice by all food handlers.

- Shower or bath daily.
- Clothing worn in a food handling area must be clean and washable.
- Hair must be clean, tied back or completely covered.
- Hands must be kept clean at all times, particularly:
  - after going to the toilet
  - before handling and serving food
  - after coughing, sneezing or blowing your nose
  - after touching your face, hair, nose, mouth and ears
  - after touching dirty surfaces or utensils or cleaning fluids
  - after handling waste food or rubbish
  - after touching raw food.
- **Fingernails** may harbour bacteria so they must be kept short and clean. Nail polish or false nails can also contaminate food and should not be worn.
- **Open cuts** must be covered with a blue waterproof plaster.
- **No jewellery** should be worn as they harbour dirt and bacteria.
- **Smoking**, **by law**, is not allowed in any food area. Cigarette ash can contaminate food, while people touching mouths and coughing cause infection.
- As **the mouth** harbours bacteria, food handlers should not eat sweets or chew gum, blow into drinking glasses to polish them or lick fingers to separate paper goods.
- To taste food use a clean teaspoon every time.
- If **people** who handle food suffer from sickness, diarrhoea, skin problems, boils or heavy colds, they must inform their teacher or supervisor. They should not prepare food that day as they may contaminate it.

Top Tip
To wash your hands you must use hot water, soap to give a good lather, making sure between your fingers, palm, back of hands and under your nails all receive attention. Rinse thoroughly in warm water, then dry with a disposable paper towel or a hot-air hand-dryer.

Quick Test

1. Name the system which organises roles and responsibilities in a professional kitchen.
2. What is the role of a Head chef in a catering establishment?
3. What is the most important requirement in the food industry?
4. Explain how to wash your hands.

Answers: 1. The partie system **2.** In charge of the kitchen, allocates work between the different kitchen sections, ensures high standards **3.** To ensure that the food which is prepared is safe to eat **4.** See Top Tip.

Kitchen hygiene

Good kitchen hygiene is the practice of maintaining high standards of cleanliness in the kitchen environment to ensure that food is safe to eat.

You must always obey some simple rules to prevent possible food poisoning and ensure good kitchen hygiene. It is a **legal requirement** that all areas where food is being stored, prepared and cooked meet the hygiene regulations of the Food Safety Act 1990 and the Food Hygiene (Scotland) Regulations 2006.

Good kitchen hygiene helps prevent food contamination; therefore the following points must be put into practice by all food handlers.

- Always ensure work surfaces, equipment and utensils are clean before you start food preparation and after use.
- Work surfaces should be easy to clean, disinfect and smooth to ensure that no bacteria or dirt can be trapped.
- Spills should be wiped up immediately – these can attract bacteria and be a safety hazard.
- Colour-coded chopping polypropylene boards should be used to prevent cross-contamination of foods being prepared.

  Red – raw meat. Brown – vegetables. Blue – fish. Yellow – cooked meats. White – bakery and dairy. Green – salad and fruit.
- Wash chopping boards, dishes and equipment in hot soapy water before starting on the next task.
- Always use clean tea towels and net cloths which must be washed at a high temperature after each use.

Top Tip
'Clean as you go.'
This means washing your dishes and cleaning your surfaces throughout practical food preparation.

- Defrost frozen foods in a suitable container in the appropriate part of the refrigerator.
- Food should be covered at all times to prevent contamination with bacteria.
- Prepare and store cooked foods away from all unprepared/raw foods to avoid risk of cross-contamination.
- A plentiful supply of hot water and cleaning materials should be available.
- All waste should be disposed of immediately and should not be allowed to accumulate at the working area.

- Waste bins should be foot operated, have well-fitting lids, be kept clean and emptied frequently.
- Toilet facilities should be located well away from food preparation areas.
- Ventilation is needed for comfortable working conditions hand to discourage bacterial growth.
- Good lighting is essential for safe working and effective cleaning.
- Any infestation of pests such as flies, vermin, should be reported immediately.
- Food stores and refuse areas must be clean and tidy.

Safety

The following points must be observed to ensure a safe working environment in the kitchen.

1. The safe use and cleaning of knives

- When carrying knives, the points must be held downwards.
- Concentrate on the job in hand as you need to work quickly and safely.
- Keep knives clean and sharp and use the correct knife for the correct purpose.
- When washing/drying sharp knives make sure the blade is away from the hand.
- Do not place sharp knives in a basin of soapy water.
- After use wash, rinse, dry and safely store the knife.
- Always ensure the chopping board is firmly anchored on the work surface by putting a damp net cloth or non slip mat underneath if necessary.

2. The safe use and cleaning of cutting machines and electrical equipment

Machines used for cutting must be thoroughly cleaned after use. Instructions for use and safety must be demonstrated to the user or instruction books made available.

Procedure for cleaning:

- Never handle plugs, electrical equipment with wet hands.
- Switch off the machine and remove the plug.
- Remove particles of food with a knife or brush.
- Clean all removable and fixed parts with hot soapy water, taking extra care with sharp parts.
- Rinse, dry and reassemble.
- Test that the equipment is properly assembled.
- Plug in and switch on.

3. The safe use of hot pots and pans

It is important to develop a sense of awareness of potential hazards in a busy kitchen.

- Pan handles should not stick out over the cooker; turn them to the side.
- Do not overfill pots or pans when cooking.
- When moving hot pans always ensure a clear passageway is available.
- Use oven gloves to carry pots and pans if the handles are hot.
- When removing a pan lid, to prevent scalding, lift the lid up and turn it over immediately.

Top Tip
Certain foods require particular care when being heated because of their high temperature, e.g. sugar, fats and oils.

Quick Test

1. What does 'clean as you go' mean?
2. Explain how you should use and clean a chopping board.
3. How would you ensure that a mixing bowl is firmly anchored to a work surface?
4. If you are unsure of how to use and clean an electrical appliance, what must you do?

Answers: 1. Washing your dishes and cleaning your surfaces throughout practical food preparation **2.** Use a separate chopping board for raw and cooked foods. Have a specific coloured board for different foods. Wash in hot soapy water after preparing each food item and anchor with a damp net cloth/non slip mat. **3.** Put a damp net cloth or non slip mat underneath the bowl. **4.** Ask your teacher/supervisor to instruct you or read the instruction book.

Storage of foods

Correct storage of foods in the kitchen is essential if contamination is to be prevented.

It is important to remember that food should be stored:

- in the correct place
- at the correct temperature
- for the correct length of time.

Cold storage

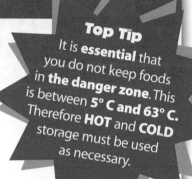

Top Tip
It is **essential** that you do not keep foods in **the danger zone**. This is between **5° C and 63° C.** Therefore **HOT** and **COLD** storage must be used as necessary.

The general rules are:

- Take extra care with the following **high-risk foods**:

  Raw meat, Poultry, Fish, Shellfish, Milk, Yoghurt, Cream cheeses Egg-based dishes (including mayonnaise), Cooked meats and pies Gravy, Cooked rice
- Raw food must always be kept separate from high-risk foods at all stages of storage and preparation to prevent contamination.
- Raw foods should be stored below cooked foods in the refrigerator.
- Always defrost poultry or meat at the bottom of the refrigerator in a suitable container which would not allow any drips to contaminate other foods.
- Rotate stored foods to lessen the risk of spoilage – first in, first out.
- Refrigerators must not be over-packed, the temperature should be checked (less than 5° C) and should also be defrosted and cleaned regularly.
- Never put hot food into the refrigerator as this will raise the temperature of other foods.
- Cool hot items as quickly as possible and then refrigerate at less than 5° C.
- Foods should be covered to prevent cross-contamination, drying out and the absorption of odours from other foods.
- When food is required to be served COLD, keep below 5° C until required.

Hot storage

The general rules are:

- If food is required to be served HOT, it must be thoroughly cooked to a minimum core temperature of 75° C.
- If food is to be reheated, it must be heated to a temperature of at least 82° C and eaten immediately.
- If food has to be kept hot until served, then a holding temperature of 63° C or above must be maintained.
- Food should only be reheated once, then thrown out.
- If in doubt, it is wiser to throw food out than risk food poisoning.

Weighing and measuring

During all food preparation, accurate weighing and measuring is essential for achieving the desired end result. In the hospitality industry, a wrong measurement of one ingredient could be a very costly mistake. The flavour, texture and appearance of the foods may all be affected.

The term 'weighing' is for dry ingredients, e.g. flour, sugar, vegetables.
The term 'measuring' is for wet ingredients, e.g. water, milk, stock.
When **weighing dry ingredients**, there are two types of scales.

Top Tip
You must always use metric measurements. Do not use handy measures – these will not give you a consistent standard of product.

Manual scales

- These scales are useful when weighing both large and small amounts of ingredients depending on the size of the scales.
- Always check that the scale pan is set onto the scales properly, the pointer is at '0' before you start and stand directly in front of the scales.
- However, they can be difficult to read.

Electronic/Digital scales

- These scales can be used to measure both small and large quantities of ingredients **accurately.** They are either battery or electronically operated.
- They must be placed on a flat surface and have a LCD display that makes them easy to read and use.
- Batteries can be expensive if they are used continually.

When **measuring wet ingredients**, there are two items of equipment which can be used.

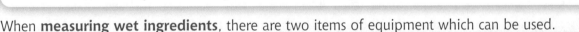

Measuring jugs

- They come in a range of sizes – the smallest being 250 ml.
- The measuring scale on a jug is usually shown in both millilitres (ml) and litres (L).
- Jugs should always be placed on a flat surface when measuring and should be read at eye level.

Measuring spoons

- These can measure small amounts of both dry ingredients and liquids.
- They come in a variety of sizes from 1.25 ml, 2.5 ml, 5 ml, 10 ml and 15 ml.
- It is a good idea to have two sets – one for use with dry ingredients, the other for liquids.

Quick Test

Complete this information.

1. Food should be stored in the correct _____, at the _____ and for the _____.
2. Give two pieces of advice for reheating food.
3. Give one disadvantage for both **a)** Manual scales and **b)** Digital scales.

Answers: 1. Place, correct temperature, correct length of time **2.** Heat to 82°C, eat immediately, reheat only once. **3. a)** They can be difficult to read: **b)** batteries can be expensive if used continually.

What's this unit all about?

In this unit you will develop knowledge of, and skills in, food preparation and culinary techniques when cooking and presenting a wide range of dishes.

There are two types of assessment for this unit.

1. Practical exercises

These cover most of Outcome 1 and all of Outcomes 2 and 3.

You will be required to complete a **folio of work.** For each practical exercise you will complete a **work record sheet**. This will form evidence for your folio which will be used for assessment.

The work record sheet will record:

- The date of the practical exercise
- The name of the dish/dishes
- The preparation techniques used
- The equipment selected
- The cookery processes undertaken
- The food used in these processes
- A description of the presentation techniques used

2. Restricted Response questions

This covers part of Outcome 1. Let's look more closely at what you have to do to be successful.

Outcomes you must complete

Outcome 1 – Prepare a range of foods using appropriate techniques and equipment

This means you have to:

- weigh and measure foods accurately
- prepare a range of foods using all the following appropriate techniques

  Blanch Skin Segment Fold Blend Strain Chop Dice Purée Pass Marinade Assemble Knead Rub in

- select appropriate equipment for the above preparation techniques
- use equipment correctly and clean it in a safe and hygienic manner
- complete a written assessment to describe the following culinary terms:

  Macedoine Jardinière Julienne Paysanne Brunoise

You will be using these culinary techniques during the practical exercises.

Outcome 2 – Cook and present a range of foods to an appropriate standard

This means you have to:

- use a range of cookery processes, both wet and dry (wet processes – boiling, poaching, stewing, steaming; dry processes – grilling, shallow frying, baking)
  You will be assessed on at least **two wet** and **two dry** cookery processes.
- use a variety of presentation techniques on your finished dishes
  Your garnish or decoration should: be the correct size related to the food being garnished/decorated; enhance the appearance of the dish; be used to indicate portions where appropriate.

Outcome 3 – Work in a safe and hygienic manner

This means you have to:

- work safely
- use hot pots and pans safely
- work hygienically
- dispose of all waste properly
- prepare raw and cooked foods separately
- secure chopping boards firmly to the work surface during use
- use hot and cold storage as necessary during the practical exercises.
- use and clean knives safely
- use electrical equipment safely
- 'clean as you go' during your practical work
- store food correctly during production

Food preparation techniques and equipment

There are a number of food preparation techniques you will learn/use during this unit when you prepare a wide range of dishes using appropriate equipment.

The first technique is to:

Assemble

What does this mean?

To put together the final dish using different prepared foods which have been part of a recipe.

Food is assembled for the following reasons:

- It is the end of the production cycle and this involves putting the final dish together.
- This technique will then allow garnishing and decoration of the dish to take place.
- It can also show portion size clearly.
- It can show the skill of a chef with an eye for detail and flair.
- It will show a standard of presentation which will enhance the final dish to make it look appetising.

Equipment required

- serving dish/plate
- large spoon
- serving ladle
- palette knife
- fish slice

Top Tip
Garnish – use additional items, e.g. tomato roses, to make savoury dishes look attractive.
Decoration – use additional items, e.g. chocolate leaves, to make sweet foods look attractive.

Top Tip
Almost all food will look best served on clean, white plates.

Quick Test

1. What are the two types of assessment which will be used in this unit?
2. What should the folio of work contain?
3. What technique is used at the end of making a lasagne?
4. Why do you think that white plates look best for serving most food?

Answers: 1. Practical exercises and Restricted Response questions **2.** A completed record sheet for each dish/dishes made during the unit – with photographs if possible **3.** Assemble **4.** White will not distract from the presentation of the food.

Blanch

What does this mean?

To plunge food into a large pan of boiling water. Bring the water back to the boil and boil for the time specified, usually 1–2 minutes. Immediately lift the food out of the water and quickly immerse the food in iced or cold water to cool quickly and stop it from cooking any further. This is called **refreshing**.

Foods are blanched for the following reasons:

- to loosen skins before skinning, e.g. tomatoes, peaches, nuts
- to preserve colour and flavour, e.g. vegetables before freezing
- to remove excess salt, e.g. in bacon, gammon
- to shorten the roasting time of vegetables, e.g. potatoes, parsnips
- to semi-cook or soften food, e.g. potatoes are softened by this process, then later fried at a high temperature to brown them prior to serving

Equipment required

- a pot – size depending on type and quantity of food being blanched
- a wire basket or sieve or slotted spoon or colander – to remove and drain the food thoroughly once blanching has been completed
- a large bowl – to hold iced or cold water

Vegetables that have been blanched can be reheated before serving by any of the following methods:

– by being dipped in boiling water

– by rapid steaming

– by being microwaved for 30–60 seconds

– by being tossed quickly in butter over a low heat

Top Tip
Slow reheating of vegetables in an oven will discolour them badly. Always use any of the above methods to reheat.

Blend

What does this mean?

To combine two or more ingredients together to form a smooth paste.

Foods are blended for the following reasons:

- to mix a dry and liquid ingredient together, e.g. starchy powder (cornflour, custard, etc) and a liquid (milk, gravy, etc) to be used in sauces
- to mix together foods which have already been cooked or do not require cooking to make a smoother texture, e.g. soups, smoothies

Equipment required

- bowl
- wooden spoon or teaspoon
- saucepan
- balloon or flat whisk
- electric blender/liquidiser for larger quantities or hand-held electric blender for smaller quantities

Top Tip

After blending a starchy powder and a measured amount of cold liquid to form a smooth paste, add the hot liquid to this mixture before returning to the heat. This will prevent lumps forming when cooking.

Electric blenders are quick and useful for making a variety of dishes such as smoothies, fruit juices, milk shakes, soups, salad dressings, sauces.

These electrical pieces of equipment can come in large industrial sizes to cope with quantities expected of large commercial kitchens.

Sauce making tip

When cooking a sauce, a whisk will continue to blend the mixture more thoroughly than a wooden spoon and help avoid lumps. In the event of a lumpy sauce, push it through a fine mesh sieve into a clean pan and then reheat it, whisking continually.

Quick Test

1. Give three reasons why vegetables are blanched.
2. What is the reason for 'refreshing' foods after blanching?
3. What equipment can be used for removing food once blanching has been completed?
4. What does the use of a whisk prevent in sauce making?
5. Name three dishes which an electric blender could help prepare?

Answers: 1. To preserve colour and flavour, to shorten the cooking time, to semi-cook or soften. **2.** To stop it from cooking any further. **3.** Wire basket, sieve, slotted spoon or colander. **4.** Lumps in the sauce. **5.** Smoothies, fruit juices, milk shakes, soups, salad dressings, sauces.

Chop

What does this mean?

To divide food into very small pieces.

Food is chopped for the following reasons:

- to roughly reduce food in size for quicker cooking, e.g. onions, meat
- for smaller particles of food for use in food preparation, e.g. nuts, tomatoes
- for finer particles of food for use as garnish, e.g. parsley, chives

Equipment required

- chopping board
- cook's knife with a sharp blade
- electrical equipment used for chopping
- food processor
- coffee grinders are ideal for chopping nuts

Top Tip

It is advisable to chop many foods by hand as electrical equipment, being fast, can over process food and reduce food to a pulp or to a finer division than required. This can happen with juicy types of vegetables like onions, leeks, celery, peppers!

When chopping, always ensure your chopping board is secure and firmly fixed on the working surface. You may need to put a damp net cloth underneath.

The action of the knife is important as it has to be efficient and safe. Use one hand to hold the food firmly and the other hand to hold and guide the knife when chopping.

The cutting action will depend on the type of food to be chopped.

Dice

What does this mean?

To cut food into small regular sized cubes, usually vegetables or meat.

Food is diced for the following reasons:

- When vegetables play a major role in a dish, they should be cut into neat shapes, e.g. dice.
- It will ensure more even cooking.

Equipment required

- chopping board
- cook's knife
- damp net cloth/non slip mat

To dice

1. If dicing a vegetable, wash, peel and wash again. If it is long and round like a carrot or courgette, cut across into pieces about 7.5 cm long. This will make dicing easier.

2. For a neat appearance, square off to give straight sides.

3. Lay the vegetable flat and cut it lengthways into uniform slices of the required thickness.

4. Arrange the strips into a row and cut across the strips into dice. The correct culinary term is **macedoine** (see Culinary Terms, page 27).

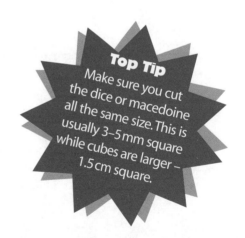

Top Tip
Make sure you cut the dice or macedoine all the same size. This is usually 3–5 mm square while cubes are larger – 1.5 cm square.

Quick Test

1. Why can electrical equipment be unsuitable for chopping?

2. Can you explain how you would chop with a cook's knife?

3. Give two reasons why food may be diced.

4. What is the culinary term for dice?

Fold

What does this mean?

To fold in – using a tablespoon or spatula, go round the outside of the bowl, cut through the centre of the mixture and turn over the mixture. This is called a figure of eight movement.

The process continues until all the ingredients are fully combined.

This technique is used in making whisked sponges and meringues.

Food is folded in for the following reasons:

- It is a gentle way of mixing ingredients, e.g. beaten egg white and caster sugar, to ensure they are evenly distributed throughout the mixture.
- It will ensure that maximum air is kept within the mixture.

Equipment required

- bowl
- tablespoon or spatula

Top Tip
Use a clear glass bowl when folding in flour to a whisked sponge mixture. This will help you check that there are no particles of flour that have not been folded in completely.

Knead

What does this mean?

To work a flour mixture such as pastry, biscuits or bread dough to remove cracks before rolling out or shaping. This can be done by hand or by an electric mixer. This technique will also add a little air to the dough, so making it lighter.

Flour mixtures are kneaded for the following reasons:

- to obtain a smooth and more elastic dough
- to get rid of cracks in scone, pastry and biscuit mixtures
- to make sure all ingredients are mixed evenly

Equipment required

- a floured board or surface
- a flour dredger
- an electric mixer with a dough hook (commercial mixers will be large and will have other attachments which can be fitted, e.g. whisk, beater)

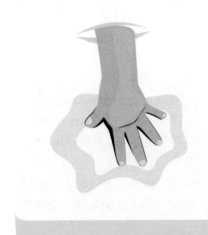

To knead bread dough

This is done by pressing the dough down with the heel of the hand, then pushing the dough forward. This process continues for 5–15 minutes until the mixture is firm, smooth and elastic. It can be a very strenuous process and in commercial kitchens it would be done by machine.

To knead scone, pastry or biscuit dough

This is a much shorter and gentler process; handle the mixture as little as possible otherwise the dough will stretch and shrink and will become hard when cooked.

Top Tip
When kneading, try to handle scone, pastry or biscuit dough with cool hands. Only the fingertips should be used.

Quick Test

1. Describe how you would fold flour into an egg and sugar mix for a whisked sponge.

2. Why is it essential to knead scone, pastry or biscuit mixture?

3. Which part of the hand do you use to knead
   a) bread dough and   b) scone mixture?

4. In commercial kitchens, why would the dough be kneaded by machine?

Answers: 1. Using a tablespoon or spatula, go round the outside the centre of the mixture and turn over the mixture. This is called a figure of eight movement. **2.** To get rid of cracks. **3.** a) Heel of the hand b) the finger tips. **4.** Because it is a strenuous process.

Marinate

What does this mean?

To cover meat or fish in a mixture (liquid or paste), usually containing oil, acid (in the form of vinegar, lemon juice or wine) and herbs and spices, before being cooked. This mixture is called a marinade.

Food is marinated for the following reasons:

- to make food more tender by using acidic ingredients such as red wine
- to add flavour by the use of herbs and spices
- to keep foods moist during cooking with the use of oil

Top Tip
There is a wide variety of exciting herbs, spices, oils, seasonings and vegetables which can be used in a marinade – be adventurous!

Equipment required

- dish or bowl to sit food in while marinating
- cover or tin foil
- tablespoon or pastry brush

The food being marinated is usually kept chilled and is turned and coated with the marinade regularly. The larger the piece of meat, the longer the process takes.

Chops, chicken drumsticks, kebabs and fish need only about 30 minutes, whereas most large roasts may need up to 24 hours. Fruit and vegetables may also be marinated.

'Dry' marinades may be used when flavouring only is required. Herbs, spices, seasonings, finely chopped onion, citrus zest are sprinkled over the food.

Pass

What does this mean?

To put a liquid or purée through a sieve or strainer to remove lumps or make it smoother. This can also be called straining (to strain).

Food is passed for the following reasons:

- to make it very smooth
- to remove seeds, lumps, seasoning, e.g. herbs
- passed food may be used for garnish or decoration and requires to be very delicate or fine, e.g. raspberry coulis

Equipment required

- fine metal sieve
- fine mesh strainer
- chinois – a conical sieve or strainer

Top Tip
A metal sieve is more efficient than a plastic one. You should also use a wooden spoon to help push the food through the sieve.

Quick Test

Complete the following crossword

Clues

Across

3. A piece of equipment used when marinating

5. A marinade does this to the food

6. A sieve should be made of this

7. An acid used in a marinade

9. A conical sieve

Down

1. Used to cover food

2. Can be a liquid or paste

4. After straining, a liquid should be _____

8. Oil is used in a marinade to keep foods in this condition

Answers: Across: 2. Tablespoon **5.** Coat **6.** Metal **7.** Lemon **9.** Chinois
Down: 1. Tinfoil **2.** Marinade **4.** Smooth **8.** Moist

Purée

What does this mean?

To mash raw or cooked food until smooth and free of lumps. This can be done by pushing the food through a sieve, or by blitzing in a liquidiser, food processor or an electric hand blender.

Food is puréed for the following reasons:

- The very smooth texture is ideal food for toddlers or convalescents.
- Plain vegetable purées are often served as accompaniments to meat, poultry or fish.
- Fruit purées are used to make sauces, coulis, soufflés, mousses and ice cream.
- Diluted with stock, vegetable purées also make fine soups, e.g. lentil soup.
- Although fruit and vegetables are most commonly used, soft fleshed meats and fish can be puréed to make stuffings, mousses or smooth patés.

Equipment required

- bowl/pot
- sieve
- food processor/liquidiser/electric blender
- spatula
- vegetable mill

To purée root vegetables

Put freshly cooked vegetables in a food processor and process until smooth, scraping down the sides of the container as necessary. Season to taste.

To purée vegetables with fibres or skin

A vegetable mill can be used to collect the fibres or skins from course vegetables, e.g. parsnips.

To purée greens

Remove the stalks from leaves before cooking, e.g. spinach. Purée in a food processor, but squeeze out as much water as possible both before and after puréeing, especially if adding cream.

Top Tip
If your soup is to be puréed, you do not need to waste a lot of time cutting the vegetables precisely.

Rub in

What does this mean?

To incorporate fat into flour for shortcrust pastry, plain biscuits and crumble toppings. This is done by rubbing the fat into the flour using the fingertips until the mixture resembles breadcrumbs. The flour particles are coated with the fat.

Rubbing in is done for the following reasons:

- to ensure the fat is distributed evenly
- to trap air in the mixture as it is lifted up – this ensures the pastry will have a lighter finished texture

Equipment required

- large baking bowl
- round bladed knife
- a pastry blender is useful if you have poor hand movement. It also helps keep the mixture cool.
- a food processor. This is a quick way to make large quantities of pastry. Take care not to go beyond the 'breadcrumb' stage.

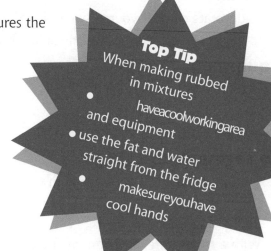

Top Tip
When making rubbed in mixtures
- haveacoolworkingarea and equipment
- use the fat and water straight from the fridge
- makesureyouhave cool hands

To rub in

1. Cut the fat into small pieces with a round bladed knife, add to the sieved flour and mix so that the fat is coated in flour.

2. Using the fingertips only, rub the fat into the flour, lifting the hands up from the bowl so that the flour falls back into the bowl and air is trapped in the mixture.

3. Shake the bowl from time to time and any lumps should come to the top of the mixture. The mixture should resemble breadcrumbs.

Top Tip
If the mixture begins to look oily, stop rubbing in, and cool the mixture in the fridge.

Quick Test

1. Why is puréed food ideal for small children?

2. What can puréed meat and fish be made into?

3. Complete the following sentence about rubbing in.
   Using the _____ of the _____, rub the _____ into the flour, lifting the _____ from the _____ so that the _____ falls back into the _____ and air is _____ in the mixture.

4. Use one word to describe what both equipment and ingredients should be before making pastry.

Segment

What does this mean?

To remove the skin and divide the flesh into segments. This is usually done with citrus fruits such as oranges and grapefruit.

Citrus fruits can be segmented for the following reasons:

- as the main ingredient in many fruit dishes, such as orange and grapefruit cocktail, salade d'oranges
- to decorate citrus flavoured sweet dishes, e.g. orange soufflé, cheesecake
- to garnish savoury dishes which contain orange in the sauce, e.g. duck à l'orange

Equipment required

- vegetable or paring knife
- bowl
- chopping board

To segment an orange

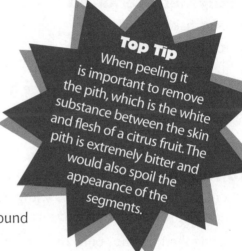

Top Tip
When peeling it is important to remove the pith, which is the white substance between the skin and flesh of a citrus fruit. The pith is extremely bitter and would also spoil the appearance of the segments.

1. Start by removing a thin slice from the top and bottom of the orange. This will allow the orange to sit steady on your chopping board.

2. With a sharp knife, and starting at the top of the orange, follow the natural shape and remove the outer skin and pith. Try not to remove the flesh as you work your way round the orange.

3. Hold the peeled fruit in your cupped palm, over a bowl, to catch the juice.

4. Working from the side of the fruit to the centre, slide the knife down one side of the membrane which protects each individual segment of the orange. Cut to release the flesh from the membrane.

5. Do the same to the other side of the segment so allowing the separated segment to fall into the bowl.

6. Continue cutting the segments, folding back the membranes like the pages of a book as you work.

7. When all the segments have been cut out, squeeze all the juice from the remaining membrane.

Skin

What does this mean?

To remove the outer skin, peel or membranes from fruit, vegetables, fish or chicken.

Foods are skinned for the following reasons:

- to improve appearance, e.g. boiled potatoes, sole fillets
- to improve the texture of a dish, e.g. skinning tomatoes for cream of tomato soup
- to make foods easier to digest, e.g. removing mango skins in fruit salad
- to improve the taste of dishes, e.g. cucumber skin can have a bitter flavour, or to allow a marinade to soak into the flesh of a chicken
- to improve the nutritional value of a dish, e.g. removing the skin from chicken will reduce the fat content

Equipment required

The equipment you use for skinning will depend on the type of food being prepared. The following could be used:

- vegetable peeler
- vegetable knife
- cook's knife
- filleting knife

Top Tip
The terms peeling and skinning are interchangeable. Peeling usually applies to fruit and vegetables. Skinning usually applies to chicken, fish and tomatoes.

To remove skins from tomatoes

1. Cut a small cross in the skin at the base of each tomato.

2. Immerse three or four at a time in boiling water.

3. Once the skins begin to curl back, in about 10 seconds, lift the tomatoes out and immerse in iced or cold water.

4. Drain and peel.

Quick Test

1. Why should the pith of citrus fruit always be removed?

2. Give two reasons why chicken should be skinned.

3. What is another technique for removing skins from tomatoes?

Answers: 1. Because it is bitter and could spoil the appearance of the segments. **2.** To reduce the fat content of the dish and to allow the marinade to soak into the flesh. **3.** Blanching

Strain

What does this mean?

To separate liquids from a solid food by pouring the mixture through a strainer.

Foods are strained for the following reasons:

- when a clear liquid is required, e.g. in jam making
- for scooping foods out of water, stock or hot fat
- for straining soups, sauces and fruits to get rid of particles, e.g. seeds of raspberries

Equipment required

There are many different types of strainers that can be used depending on the type of food being prepared.

- a sieve for rice, vegetables
- a chinois – a conical metal sieve used by professional chefs for straining stocks, sauces, creams and jellies
- colander for vegetables, pasta
- basket strainer for scooping food items out of hot fat, water or stock

- steel funnel with strainer – ideal for removing small food particles from cooking oil
- muslin, which is a very thin cotton material, can be used when a very clear liquid is required, e.g. in jam and jelly making

Top Tip
Many dishes are enhanced by garnishing or decorating with a very smooth sauce, the result of careful straining of liquids, e.g. fruit coulis.

Culinary terms

There are **five** culinary terms of vegetable cuts you need to know and practise throughout this unit.

Cut of vegetable	Definition
Julienne	Thin strips 1 mm thick × 20 mm in length **How to cut** – Fine slices then fine strips
Brunoise	Very small dice 2 mm × 2 mm × 2 mm if using as part of a recipe for soup. 1 mm × 1 mm × 1 mm if using for a garnish **How to cut** – As for julienne then across into very fine dice
Jardinière	Batons 3 mm × 3 mm × 18 mm but sometimes in the hospitality industry batons are cut 5 mm × 5 mm × 15 mm. **How to cut** – Cut to 18 mm lengths, square up. 3 mm slice then 3 mm strip
Macedoine	Small cubed dice 3 mm × 3 mm × 3 mm or 5 mm × 5 mm × 5 mm **How to cut** – As for jardinière then into dice
Paysanne	Thin flat cut of triangles, squares or rounds 1 cm sided triangles 1 cm sided squares 1 cm diameter rounds

Top Tip Depending on the catering kitchen, the exact sizes of these cuts can vary. It is important, whatever the size of the cut, that the vegetables are the correct shape and all equal sizes.

Top Tip Remember these links – julienne can be cut into brunoise, jardinière can be cut into macedoine.

Quick Test

1. Why are foods strained?
2. What is a chinois?
3. What are the culinary terms for a) small dice b) batons c) thin strips d) very small dice e) flat cut of vegetable, either triangles, squares or rounds?

Answers: 1. When a clear liquid is required or to get rid of particles. **2.** A conical metal sieve used by professional chefs for straining stocks, sauces, creams and jellies. **3. a)** macedoine **b)** jardinière **c)** julienne **d)** brunoise **e)** paysanne

Presentation techniques

Top Tip
Photograph some of your best work and keep in your folio as evidence of your work.

Garnishes and decorations

The presentation of food is helped by using appropriate garnishing or decoration techniques. There are a number of reasons why we garnish and decorate foods:

- to enhance the appearance of the dish
- to indicate portion size. Pepperoni has been used to garnish this pizza. Twelve pepperoni slices have been arranged on the outside of the pizza showing where it can be portioned equally for four people, allowing each person three slices of pepperoni.
- to complement the flavour, colour, texture, shape and size of finished dishes

It is important to remember that garnishes and decorations should be:

- appropriate to the foods being cooked
- the correct size in relation to the foods being served
- edible and served as fresh as possible.

Here are a few simple garnishes and decorations for you to practise.

Top Tip
Garnishes are usually edible, brightly coloured items for **savoury** dishes.
Decorations are usually edible items for **sweet** dishes – either simple or ornate.

Garnishes for savoury dishes

Parsley

Fresh parsley can be an effective bright, colourful garnish for savoury dishes.
It can be:

Chopped

Wash parsley and dry well in a paper towel. Place on a chopping board, discard the stalks and with a very sharp cook's knife, keeping the point of the blade firmly on the board, chop backwards and forwards until the parsley is finely chopped. Sprinkle over the dish or in centre of dish.

Parsley en branche

Wash a stalk of parsley and pat it dry. Select a sprig whose size and shape is in keeping with the dish. Place on top of the dish.

Top Tip
Fresh mint can be used in the same way in both sweet and savoury dishes.

Tomato

Always use firm ripe tomatoes when garnishing savoury dishes. Here are a few ideas:

Tomato concassé (or coarsely chopped tomato)

Skin tomato by plunging into boiling water.

Halve the tomato and remove the seeds.

Chop into neat small dice.

Tomato slices/wedges

Sometimes simple slices cut across the tomato are an ideal decoration.

Equally, tomato wedges can be used. Always cut off the white stalk area.

Tomato roses

Using a small sharp paring knife, turn the firm, ripe tomato upside down and make an incision in the base of the tomato. Peel the skin off thinly – 1.5 cm wide and in a continuous strip. Assemble into a rose by twisting the skin around. Have the skin side out. Fix the end in to hold.

Top Tip
Roses can also be made from citrus fruit peel.

Tomato Van Dyke

Use a firm tomato and hold with the stalk at the top. Insert the point of a sharp vegetable knife at an angle of 45 degrees half way down the tomato and make a cut into the centre. Repeat this action around the centre of the tomato in a zigzag formation until you have gone right round. Give a sharp twist to separate.

Quick Test

1. Give three reasons why food is garnished or decorated.

2. State two ways parsley could be used as a garnish.

3. Explain how you would prepare tomato concassé.

Answers: 1. To enhance the appearance of the dish; to indicate portion size; to complement the flavour, colour, texture, shape and size of food dishes. **2.** Chopped and en branche. **3.** Skin tomato by plunging into boiling water. Halve the tomato and remove the seeds. Chop into small neat dice.

Cucumber

Cucumber twists

With a potato peeler take small slivers alternately down the length of a piece of cucumber then slice. Cut down the slice slightly beyond the centre and twist. These twists can be laid on top of one another or side by side.

Cucumber ribbons

Cut a length of cucumber and take off thin slivers using a potato peeler. The first few slivers can be discarded as they will contain too much skin. Manipulate into twists, folded or draped over one another

Cucumber fan

Cut a diagonal length of cucumber approximately 2.5 cm. Using a sharp vegetable or cook's knife cut very thin slices, almost completely through. Leave attached by the outer skin only. Spread out and arrange in a fan shape.

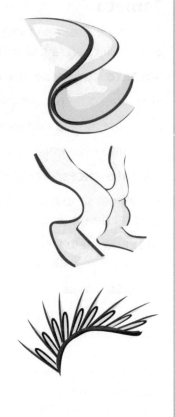

Spring onion curls

This garnish is ideal for rice dishes but has to be made in advance as it takes time to form.

Cut off the root and outer skin.

Cut off a length of approximately 4–5 cm from the root end.

Come up about ½ cm from the root end and cut about 6–8 times towards the cut end, rotating the spring onion as you do it so that the cuts are evenly placed.

Place in a bowl of cold water in the fridge. It will be ready when the tips start to curl.

Fruit and herbs

From a small bunch of shiny blackcurrants to a generous sprig of bright green, fresh mint – the options are endless. However, ensure your choice complements the flavours and textures of your dish. All fruit and herbs must be at their freshest or they will spoil the presentation and cause customers to question the freshness of the overall dish.

Top Tip
When preparing garnishing items for hot dishes, they must be prepared in advance, then placed on the food as quickly as possible so that the dish does not cool down.

Citrus fruits

These fruits are ideal for many culinary garnishes or decorations. Many variations can be made from lemons, oranges and limes such as wedges, slices and twists.

Wedges

Wash fruit and halve by cutting down vertically.

Cut into wedges of appropriate size.

Remove any stones and pith at the centre and top of wedge.

Slices/twists

Wash fruit, and with a very sharp knife, cut thin slices.

Cut from slightly above the centre to the edge of each slice.

Gently twist the fruit from the slit in opposite directions.

These can be used singly, together or side by side.

Citrus butterfly

Using the end cut of a citrus fruit, prepare two thin strips for antennae.

Cut a thin slice of the fruit in half and then in half again but not right through to the centre. Space out to form wings – the centre should still be attached.

Citrus zest strips

Using a vegetable peeler, shave off the topmost layer, i.e. the zest, from orange, lemon or lime peel in wide strips.

With a sharp knife, cut the peel into narrow strips (julienne).

A combination of citrus fruit peel makes a very effective decoration.

Top Tip

See page 24 'To segment an orange' which is another variation of using citrus fruits as a garnish or decoration.

Slices with a loop

Cut a slice of fruit and cut round the fruit where the flesh and the pith meet. Only cut ¾ of the way round the fruit.

Tie the peel strip in a loop.

Quick Test

1. How would you prepare an orange twist?

2. What three citrus fruits would make attractive zest strips?

3. State two points to consider when choosing herbs to improve the presentation of your dish.

Answers: 1. Wash fruit and with a very sharp knife, cut thin slices. Cut from slightly above the centre to the edge of each slice. Gently twist the fruit from the slits in the opposite direction. **2.** Oranges, lemons and limes. **3.** They must be fresh. They must complement the flavour and texture of the dish.

Decorations for sweet dishes

Fruit coulis

These are sauces made with tinned, fresh or cooked fruits and caster or icing sugar puréed together.

- Red fruit and berries are often used for their intense colour.
- Those containing pips such as raspberries and strawberries should be puréed and sieved.
- Mango, apricot and kiwis are also good for their bright colour.
- Often two colours of coulis will be used on the same plate for contrast.
- A simple technique is to feather a pattern using a cocktail stick to draw one coulis through the other.
- Feathering is also effective with cream and a dark coulis.

The following patterns can also be created

Top Tip
Practise any patterns on a plate before you do it on your serving dish.

Drag

Place four drops of coulis in descending size.

Use a skewer to drag across the middle of each drop of coulis.

Swirl

When doing a swirl of coulis, start in the middle. This will give you more control.

Zigzag

This can be done across the plate before placing a portion of dessert on the plate. Alternatively the zigzag can be placed beside the portion.

Strawberry fans

Wash fruit and leave the stalk on.

Lay the strawberry on its side and with a sharp knife, cut strips slightly down from the top to the tip.

Use fingers to spread out and then place as decoration.

Top Tip
If the strawberry is large cut in half from the stalk down before fanning.

Cream

Cream can add a simple or ornate look to both savoury and sweet dishes. It can be used for:

Swirls

A fine swirl of cream can be effective on the top of soup.

Rosettes of cream

Whip double or whipping cream until it will stand firmly in peaks.

Place star tube into a piping bag. Place this into a measuring jug and fold the top of the bag over the top of the measuring jug. Spoon in the cream.

Twist the top of the bag until there is no air left in the piping bag.

Hold the bag upright, just above the surface of the item to be piped.

Squeeze out some cream, moving the bag in a small circle. Stop squeezing before you lift the nozzle away. Press down lightly and pull the piping bag up sharply.

Top Tip

A swirl of cream on soup can be made more exciting by feathering – take a cocktail stick and drag out the sides at even intervals.

Quick Test

1. What can fruit coulis be made from?

2. How would you prepare a strawberry fan?

3. Describe the correct way to fill a piping bag.

Answers: 1. Tinned, fresh or cooked fruits and caster or icing sugar puréed together. **2.** Wash fruit and leave the stalk on. Lay the strawberry on its side and with a sharp knife, cut strips slightly down from the top to the tip. Use fingers to spread out and then place on as decoration. **3.** Place star tube into a piping bag. Place this into a measuring jug and fold the top of the bag over the top of the measuring jug. Spoon in the cream.

Chocolate

Chocolate can be a very versatile decoration for sweet items. It can be:

Grated

Use either large or small grater holes with chocolate that has been refrigerated.

Curled

To make chocolate curls, have chocolate at room temperature. Use a vegetable peeler to shave off long curls onto a sheet of greaseproof paper. Tip the curls straight onto the dessert from the paper.

Shaped

Chocolate can be melted and piped into a shape using a small writing pipe. This can be done on tinfoil and left to harden; then carefully peeled off.

Chocolate can be melted onto greaseproof paper and once set can be cut into shapes using a sharp knife.

Melted chocolate can be spread onto clean bubble wrap and left to set. It can then be peeled of and broken carefully into pieces and used to decorate desserts.

Icing sugar/cocoa powder

This is an extremely easy and simple decoration. Powders can be sieved separately or together to remove lumps. Use a fine sieve to gently dust the top of the dessert or, for effect, an area of a plate with the powder.

Additional ideas on garnishing and decorating can be found at **www.leckieandleckie.co.uk** by clicking on the **Learning Lab** button and navigating to the *Intermediate 2 Hospitality Success Guide* page.

Top Tip
To save time a variety of chocolate shapes can be purchased from the supermarket – leaves, cigarillo shapes and flat marbled squares.

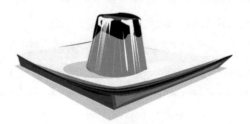

Quick Test

1. Name three ways of using chocolate as a decoration.
2. How should chocolate be stored if it is going to be **(a)** grated and **(b)** curled?
3. State three ways of using melted chocolate as a decoration.

Answers: 1. Grated, curled and shapes. **2. (a)** in a refrigerator **(b)** at room temperature. **3. (1)** Piped into shapes **(2)** Cut into shapes **(3)** Spread onto clean bubble wrap, left to set and then peeled off.

Assessment practice

To help you pass the assessment for Practical Cookery Skills for the Hospitality Industry complete the following activities:

1. Match each of the following culinary terms with its description.

Culinary term	Description
A Macedoine	**1** 3 mm × 3 mm × 18 mm length
B Jardinière	**2** 1 cm in size
C Julienne	**3** 5 mm × 5 mm × 5 mm
D Paysanne	**4** 2 mm × 2 mm × 2 mm
E Brunoise	**5** 1 mm × 20 mm length

Answers

A ☐ B ☐ C ☐ D ☐ E ☐

2. The following questions on food preparation techniques will help you during your practical assessments.

   a. What is the technique used to put together the final dish using different prepared foods which have been part of a recipe?

   b. After food is blanched in boiling water, what must you do to stop it from cooking any further?

   c. If you are making a cheese sauce and it becomes lumpy, what should you do?

   d. Explain how you would cut **dice** from a carrot.

   e. Name two dishes which require the technique **fold** in their making.

   f. In making the biscuit base for strawberry shortcake, why would you knead the mixture?

   g. Fill in the following spaces
   Food is marinated to make it more _____, to add _____, to keep foods _____ during cooking.

   h. After fat has been rubbed into flour what should the mixture resemble?

   i. Name four pieces of equipment which may be used to 'skin' food.

   j. Suggest a garnish or decoration which would be suitable for the following dishes:

   – cream of tomato soup

   – fish pie

   – strawberry cheesecake

What's this unit all about?

In this unit you will develop knowledge and skills in selecting ingredients and methods of preparing and cooking foods with the purpose of producing dishes which will promote healthier eating.

There are three types of assessment for this unit.

1. **Written exercises** – selection and amendment, planning and costing exercises
   This covers Outcome 1.

2. **A written short answer exercise**
   This covers Outcome 2.

3. **Practical activity**
   This covers Outcome 3.

Let's look more closely at what you have to do to be successful.

Outcomes you must complete

Outcome 1 – Identify and amend the recipes for a range of established dishes to provide a healthier end product

This means you have to:

- Select **three recipes** in total, each one from a **different** category from the following list:
  Soup, quiche/pie, pasta dish with sauce, chicken dish, ethnic dish, salad and dressing, savoury dish using potatoes/vegetables, hot/cold sweet and accompanying sauce, cake/pastry.
- Make **two** amendments to **each** recipe to provide a healthier end product.
- Provide a work plan for **each** dish you have selected.
- Undertake a costing exercise for a prescribed dish (this is a recipe provided by SQA).

Outcome 2 – Identify and evaluate methods of cookery that enhance healthier eating

This means you have to:

- Identify **three** cookery methods that will produce a healthier end product.
- Give two explanations why **each** method of cookery was selected.

Outcome 3 – Using the amended recipes, produce a range of dishes to promote healthier eating

This means you have to:

- Use preparation techniques and cooking methods which are appropriate and will maximise retention of nutrients.
- Produce the dishes within a given timescale.
- Present the dishes to an appropriate standard.
- Demonstrate safe and hygienic practices during food preparation.

Ingredients for healthy eating

With Scotland's poor health record of obesity, heart disease, high blood pressure, diabetes and cancer, it has never been so important to have a balanced diet, both at home and in the hospitality industry.

'The Eatwell plate' can be used to encourage us to eat a range of food and so achieve a more balanced, healthy diet.

The Eatwell plate

Top Tip
The size of each section of the plate illustrates the proportion of that food group you should be eating daily.

The Eatwell plate is divided into five food group sections:

1. Fruit and vegetables
2. Bread, rice, potatoes, pasta (and other starchy foods)
3. Milk and dairy foods
4. Meat, fish, eggs and beans (and other non dairy sources of protein)
5. Foods and drinks high in fat and/or sugar

The sections of the Eatwell plate show that the majority of our foods should be taken from Section 1 – fruit and vegetables and Section 2 – bread, rice, potatoes and pasta. The section we should be eating least of is Section 5 – foods and drinks high in fat and/or sugar.

Top Tip
Salt is found in some of the foods in the Eatwell plate. We should be cutting down on salt intake.

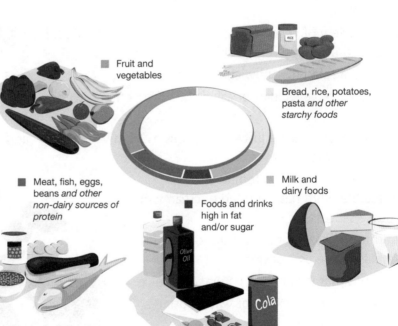

Fruit and vegetables

Bread, rice, potatoes, pasta *and other starchy foods*

Meat, fish, eggs, beans *and other non-dairy sources of protein*

Foods and drinks high in fat and/or sugar

Milk and dairy foods

Quick Test

1. Name four dietary diseases that can be caused by not eating a balanced diet.
2. Which two food groups should we be eating more of?
3. Which group should we be eating less of?

Fruit and vegetables

Why eat fruit and vegetables?

- They are important sources of anti-oxidant vitamins A, C and E.
- They are low in calories.
- Almost all are fat free.
- They provide a good source of fibre.

What is a portion?

- 150 ml unsweetened fruit juice
- 3 heaped tablespoons of vegetables or fruit salad
- a handful of grapes, cherries or berries
- 1 banana, apple, orange or 2 plums or similar sized fruit
- 1 bowl salad
- 1 bowl home made soup
- 1 tablespoon of dried fruit

How can we improve fruit and vegetable intake?

- Add extra vegetables to pizza toppings, curries, casseroles, stews or stir fries.
- Use a variety of vegetables in soups – soups can be liquidised to get rid of lumpy vegetables.
- Add extra salad to sandwiches.
- Two types of vegetables or salad should be offered with each main meal.
- Frozen vegetables are just as nutritious as fresh vegetables – and sometimes even more so.
- Serve sauces based on tomatoes or vegetables with pasta instead of creamy or cheese sauces.
- Add fresh, frozen or dried fruit to breakfast cereals or use as a dessert.
- Use fruit that is tinned in natural fruit juice.
- Smoothies are an excellent way of using a variety of fruit and are very popular with children.
- Add dried fruit such as apricots, cranberries, sultanas to baking, breakfast cereals and to desserts.

Top Tip
Anti-oxidant vitamins will help to prevent heart disease and some cancers so try to eat **five portions of fruit and vegetables a day.**

What is a portion?

Top Tip
Dried fruit can contain a high amount of sugar so only add a tablespoon to breakfast cereals.

Bread, rice, potatoes, pasta (and other starchy foods)

Starchy carbohydrate foods such as bread, rice, potatoes, pasta and cereals are a very important part of a healthy diet. You should try to have at least two servings of this group **every day, at each meal.**

Why eat bread, cereals, rice, potatoes and pasta?

- Starchy carbohydrates are a good source of slow-release energy.
- They are low in fat.
- They provide minerals such as calcium and iron.
- They supply the vitamin B group.
- They are a good source of fibre if the wholegrain varieties are eaten.

What is a portion?

- 1 bowl of breakfast cereal – the wholegrain variety
- 1 slice of bread – preferably wholemeal or wholegrain variety
- 1 medium potato – but not in the form of chips or roast potatoes
- 2 tablespoons of cooked rice or pasta – preferably the wholemeal variety

What is a portion?

How can we improve bread, cereals, rice, potatoes, and pasta intake?

- Breakfast cereals should be high fibre, low sugar varieties. These can also be used in desserts such as fruit crumbles, biscuits, e.g. porridge oats.
- Use wholemeal flour when cooking and baking instead of white.
- Different types of bread such as wholemeal breads, wholemeal pitta breads, granary rolls and bagels should be used in sandwiches.
- Potatoes should be mashed using low fat spreads and skimmed milk.
- Potatoes should be baked or boiled with the skin on.
- Add pasta or rice to soups to make them more filling.
- Serve rice boiled or steamed. Avoid fried rice such as pilau and egg fried rice.
- Brown rice and wholemeal pasta should be used to increase fibre content.

Top Tip
Starchy foods contain less than half the calories of fat. You need to watch for added fat during cooking or serving.

Quick Test

1. Thinking of a balanced diet, which of the following foods – A or B – should you choose and why?
   1 **A** Fruit tinned in syrup   **B** Fruit tinned in natural juice
   2 **A** Egg fried rice   **B** Boiled rice
   3 **A** White rolls   **B** Wholemeal rolls
   4 **A** Dried apricots   **B** Fresh apricots

2. Why are the vitamins A, C and E found in fruit and vegetables important to our health?

3. What are the 'healthier' methods of serving potatoes?

Milk and dairy foods

This section includes foods such as milk, yoghurt, cheese, cream, fromage frais, crème fraiche.

Why eat milk and dairy foods?

- They provide protein for growth and repair of body tissues and cells.
- They are a good source of calcium which helps the development and maintenance of strong bones and teeth.
- They provide vitamins A, D and B12.

What is a portion?

- 200 ml milk
- 125 ml yoghurt
- 30 g cheese
- 50 ml cream, fromage frais, crème fraiche

Make best choices of milk and dairy foods

- Use lower fat versions of this food group such as semi-skimmed or skimmed milk, low fat yoghurts, cream, fromage frais or crème fraiche.
- Use plain yoghurt, fromage frais or crème fraiche instead of cream or sour cream in recipes.
- Fruit flavoured yoghurt could be changed to plain yoghurt with fresh fruit added.
- Use low fat spread instead of butter for spreading.
- If using cheese to flavour a dish use a very strong tasting cheese such as Red Leicester or blue cheese because less will be needed to give taste.
- Use fat reduced cheese such as Edam or cottage cheese.

What is a portion?

fromage

milk

Top Tip

Dairy foods can contain saturated fat, which can raise cholesterol and increase the risk of heart disease. Some are high in salt which can cause high blood pressure, strokes and heart disease. For these reasons the amount eaten of this food group should be carefully controlled.

Meat, fish, eggs and pulses (and other non dairy sources of protein)

You should try to have **two servings daily.**

Why eat meat, fish, eggs and pulses?

- These foods are all good sources of protein, which is needed for growth and repair of tissues.
- Meat contains iron and vitamin B group including B12.
- White fish is low in fat.
- Oily fish are a good source of vitamins A and D. They are also rich in Omega 3 which will reduce the risk of heart disease.
- Fish where the bones are eaten, e.g. salmon, are good sources of calcium and phosphorous.
- Pulses including lentils, beans such as kidney, butter and soya, peas are low in fat, high in fibre, contain iron and add extra protein.
- Use meat alternatives such as mycoprotein (Quorn), tofu and textured vegetable protein. These plant sources are usually low in fat and good sources of fibre.

Top Tip
White fish contains very little fat but do not fry it coated in breadcrumbs, batter or creamy sauce as these will increase the fat of the dish. Try to steam, grill, poach or microwave.

What is a portion?

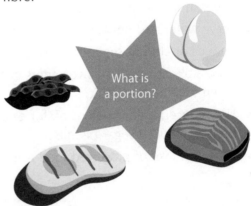

What is a portion?

- 60 g cooked lean meat or poultry
- 90 g cooked fish
- 2 eggs
- 90 g beans

How can we improve the intake of meat, fish, eggs and pulses?

- Use lean cuts of meat, extra lean minced beef and trim excess fat from meat.
- Remove the skin from poultry before cooking to reduce fat.
- Use methods of cooking which will reduce the fat content, e.g. grilling.
- Add pulses to meat dishes to increase the fibre content, reduce the fat and add extra protein.

Quick Test

1. Which nutrients are found in milk and dairy foods?

2. What is the effect on our health if too many dairy foods are eaten?

3. Are the following statements true or false?

   a) Adding lentils to meat dishes will increase the fibre content.

   b) Leaving the skin on chicken will reduce the fat content.

   c) Oily fish is a good source of Omega 3.

   d) Tofu and textured vegetable protein are plant sources of protein.

Answers: 1. Protein, calcium, vitamins A, D and B12. **2.** They can raise cholesterol and increase the risk of heart diseases. Some can be high in salt which can cause high blood pressure, strokes and heart disease. **3. a)** True **b)** False **c)** True **d)** True

Foods and drinks high in fat and/or sugar

Foods containing fats and sugars are often eaten in greater quantities than is needed by the body and this can result in obesity, heart disease, high blood pressure and diabetes. Sugar snacks and drinks taken regularly throughout the day are a major cause of tooth decay.

Why eat this group?

- Polyunsaturated fats contain essential fatty acids such as Omega 3.
- Margarines are fortified with vitamins A and D.
- Sugar will give you a quick burst of energy but starchy food will give a slow release of energy which is better for your health.

How can we decrease fat and sugar intake?

- Choose a low fat spread or a polyunsaturated fat instead of butter.
- Use unsaturated oils such as olive, sunflower or rape seed oils in preference to butter or margarine when cooking.
- Use fat free or reduced calories salad dressings.
- Use 'Fry Light' olive oil spray when sweating vegetables.
- Change the pastry topping of a savoury pie to mashed potato as this is lower in fat.
- Serve water and unsweetened fruit juices instead of sugary drinks.
- Reduce or cut out sugar in tea or coffee or use artificial sweeteners.
- If possible use artificial sweeteners or half sugar when cooking, e.g. when stewing fresh fruit.
- Use reduced sugar versions of, for example, jam for spreading on breads, reduced sugar biscuits.
- Reduce intake of processed food as these can contain high amounts of fat and sugar.

Top Tip
Health warning!! Fat, sugar and salt are the main causes of many diet-related diseases if too much is eaten.

Salt

Salt can be found in many foods identified in the Eatwell plate. Adding salt to food and eating foods high in salt can contribute to raised blood pressure and to heart disease and strokes.

How can we decrease intake of salt

- Use herbs and spices to flavour foods.
- Use 'Lo Salt'.
- Always taste food before adding salt. This can be during the cooking process or when serving.
- Use reduced salt versions of foods, e.g. baked beans, peas, gravy granules.
- Use 'lower in salt' stock cubes or make your own stock using vegetables.
- Limit the use of soy sauce or change to low salt soy sauce.
- Choose tuna in spring water rather than in brine or sunflower oil.

Top Tip
Approximately 75% of the salt we eat is already in the processed food we eat. It is better to prepare foods from scratch as the amount of salt added can be controlled.

Amending recipes

The ingredients in many recipes can be adapted without affecting the taste or texture of the food. This can be done by

- **reducing the amount of**:
- fat, e.g. when sautéing vegetables use less oil and a non stick pan;
- sugar, e.g. reduce the sugar and add spices such as cinnamon, cloves for flavour;
- salt, e.g. use less soy sauce – which contains a lot of salt – in the recipe;
- **making a healthy substitution,** e.g. use skimmed milk to make a sauce instead of full fat milk.

Look at the following ingredients for **Savoury Macaroni and Cheese.**

50 g macaroni

25 g margarine

25 g plain flour

250 ml milk

75 g mild Cheddar cheese

50 g streaky bacon

½ teaspoon salt

Now look at how the ingredients can be changed in order to make **Healthier Macaroni and Cheese.**

Macaroni can be changed to wholemeal macaroni.

Margarine can be changed to polyunsaturated margarine.

Cheese can be changed to a smaller amount of stronger Red Leicester cheese.

Milk can be changed to semi-skimmed milk.

Streaky bacon can be changed to a trimmed back bacon rasher.

Salt can be changed to 'Lo Salt'.

Top Tip
To reduce the fat content of a sauce, it could be made with cornflour and semi-skimmed milk so no margarine would be required.

Quick Test

1. Alter the ingredients of the following recipes to make them healthier.

Fruit Crumble

Base:
200 g cooking apples,
50 g sugar

Topping:
125 g plain flour,
50 g margarine,
50 g sugar,
2.5 ml mixed spice

Curried Rice Salad

5 ml salt
50 g rice
25 g margarine for frying vegetables
50 g green peppers
50 g red peppers
50 g onions
75 ml salad cream
5 ml curry powder
25 g Cheddar cheese

2. Why should the intake of processed foods be reduced?

3. Which type of fats should be used instead of butter?

Answers
1. Fruit Crumble: Reduce sugar or change to artificial sweetener or half sugar – either no sugar or less will be needed. Change cooking apples to eating apples. Change sugar in topping or add dried fruit such as sultanas to topping. Margarine could be reduced slightly. Wholemeal flour, porridge oats or muesli in topping. **Curried Rice Salad:** Rice should be brown rice. Change margarine to sunflower oil for frying or use 'Fry Light' olive oil. Reduced fat salad cream could be used. No salt is needed as curry powder will flavour. **2.** They can contain a high amount of fat, sugar and salt. **3.** Low fat spread, polyunsaturated margarine, olive oil, sunflower or rape seed oil

Preparation techniques for healthy eating

Using correct food preparation techniques can help to promote a healthy diet. Let's look at each section of the Eatwell plate.

1. Fruit and vegetables

Vitamin C and the B group are water soluble vitamins and can be very easily lost from fruit and vegetables during preparation. So how can this be prevented?

- Avoid peeling if possible or remove a thin skin only, because vitamins are often found close to the skin. The skin will also provide a source of fibre in the diet.
- Never leave vegetables soaking in water as the water soluble vitamins can leach (leak) out and be lost.
- Do not cut the fruit or vegetables into small pieces as it exposes more surface area for vitamins to be lost into the air.
- Fruit and vegetables should be prepared using sharp knives because blunt edges cause an enzyme within the food to react causing bruising and a loss of vitamin C.
- Prepare fruit and vegetables just before they are needed because vitamins can be lost into the air.

Top Tip
Oxidation is the correct term when vitamins are lost into the air.

2. Bread, rice, potatoes, pasta (and other starchy foods)

- When you are sieving wholemeal flour, always empty the contents of the sieve into the bowl as the husks which are left are full of fibre and vitamins.
- Choose wholegrain varieties of pasta and rice as these contain more fibre.

3. Milk and dairy foods

- As an alternative to double cream, use a mixture of half yoghurt and half cream to lower the fat content.

4. Meat, fish, eggs and pulses (and other non dairy sources of protein)

- Remove all visible fat from meat before cooking.
- Skim fat from stews, soups before serving.
- Drain surface fat from food before serving by blotting with absorbent paper or kitchen roll.
- Meat alternatives such as soya, tofu and quorn can be used as they are low in fat.

5. Foods and drinks high in fat and/or sugar

- If frying foods ensure that the oil is at the correct temperature as this reduces the amount of fat which is absorbed.
- Puréed vegetables can be used to thicken sauces instead of making sauces from flour and margarine.
- Baked foods can be sweetened by using dried fruits. This reduces the amount of sugar.

Top Tip

Manufacturers and the hospitality industry are responding to consumers' interest in healthier eating by giving clearer labelling on packaging, e.g. the traffic light system, and indicating the healthier options on menus.

Quick Test

A The following crossword contains words that are all associated with food preparation techniques which can help promote a healthy diet.

Clues

Down

1. Avoid doing this to vegetables if possible

3. Knives should be this to prevent bruising

4. Water soluble vitamins will leach out if vegetables are left doing this for too long

5. Easily lost during preparation

Across

2. _____ soluble vitamins can be easily lost

6. Vitamins getting lost into the air

7. To remove fat from the top of stews

8. Type of fruit added which will allow the amount of sugar to be reduced

B Why should oil be at the correct temperature **before** adding food to be fried?

C Why should fruit or vegetables not be cut into too small pieces?

D Why should fruit and vegetables be prepared just before serving?

Answers: A Down: 1. Peeling 3. Sharp 4. Soaking 5. Vitamins.
Across: 2. Water 6. Oxidation 7. Skim 8. Dried.
B So that the amount of fat that is absorbed is reduced. **C** Because this exposes more surface area for vitamins to be lost into the air.
D Because vitamins can be lost into the air.

Cookery methods for healthy eating

How we cook our food can help to produce a healthier end product.

Methods of cooking can be classified as:

Wet methods – heat is applied through water or some other liquid and this is used to cook the food. This includes boiling, stewing, pot roasting, poaching, braising and steaming.

Dry methods – do not require the use of a liquid. This includes baking, grilling, roasting, stir frying and microwaving. Stir frying is a dry method of cooking as the oil or fat does not contain water.

Wet methods of cooking

Boiling This is cooking food in a liquid such as water, milk or stock. This can be either:
– a quick and rapid process, e.g. when boiling vegetables
– a slower process called simmering used for rice, pasta, minced meat, potatoes.

How it contributes to healthy eating	Link to health
No fat is added during this method.	The reduction in fat lowers the risks of obesity and heart disease.
The addition of salt can be controlled.	The reduction in salt lowers the risk of high blood pressure, heart disease and strokes.
In the case of soups and stews, all the food is served.	If additional vegetables are added to stews and soups then fibre is increased, which prevents constipation, bowel disorders.
Although there will be some nutrient loss, especially water soluble vitamins, the liquid can be used for making stock or soup. If food is placed in a minimum amount of boiling water this reduces the cooking time.	Retains the nutritional value, e.g. vitamin C in green vegetables, which will contribute to general good health.

Stewing This involves cooking food slowly and gently in a pan with a tight fitting lid, using a small quantity of liquid such as water or stock. Suitable foods include meat, poultry, vegetables, fruit.

How it contributes to healthy eating	Link to health
Visible fat from the meat and poultry can be trimmed off before cooking.	The reduction in fat lowers the risk of obesity, heart disease.
No additional fat is added.	
Water soluble vitamins will not be lost as the food and the liquid from the stew are served together.	Retains the nutritional value, e.g. vitamin C in vegetables, which will contribute to general good health.
A complete meal can be made in one container using a wide range of nutritious foods such as vegetables.	Vegetables will add vitamin C and fibre to the dish. Fibre prevents constipation and bowel disorders.

Poaching This involves covering the food in the minimum amount of liquid and cooking gently. In most cases the food is placed in the simmering water, e.g. eggs, whole fish, fruit.

How it contributes to healthy eating	Link to health
No fat is added so the food is healthier.	The reduction in fat lowers the risk of obesity and heart disease.
Water soluble vitamins may leach into the cooking liquid, but if this is served with the food, nutrient loss is reduced.	
Minimum cooking time and water are used, so nutrient loss is minimised.	Vitamins are retained which will contribute to general good health.

Braising This involves cooking foods such as meat, chicken, vegetables in the oven in a covered container with stock or liquid. Braised food is usually placed on a bed of vegetables before being 2/3 covered with liquid.

How it contributes to healthy eating	Link to health
Little or no fat is used.	This lowers the risk of obesity, heart disease.
There will be some loss of water soluble vitamins but in some cases the cooking liquid is served as a gravy/sauce.	Vitamins are retained which will contribute to general good health.
Vegetables are added and so contribute to healthy eating.	Vegetables will add fibre to the dish which prevents constipation and bowel disorders.

Steaming This method involves cooking food in the steam rising from boiling water. Suitable foods include fish, vegetables, sweet puddings.

How it contributes to healthy eating	Link to health
No fat is required in this method so the end product is healthier and easier to digest.	The reduction in fat lowers the risk of obesity, heart disease.
Fewer nutrients – vitamins C and B group – are lost as food does not come into direct contact with water.	Vitamins are retained which will contribute to general good health.
It is a very suitable method for vegetables as no salt is needed as the flavour is kept.	The reduction in salt lowers the risk of high blood pressure, heart disease and strokes.
Vegetables are also a valuable source of fibre.	This helps prevents bowel disorders.

Quick Test

1. Explain the difference between wet and dry methods of cooking.
2. Why are fewer nutrients lost by the steaming method of cooking?
3. Why should you use the cooking liquid that has been used for braising meat for gravy?
4. Why should you add vegetables to boiling water?

Answers: 1. In wet methods heat is applied through water or some other liquid and this is used to cook the food. Dry methods do not require the use of a liquid. **2.** Because food does not come into direct contact with water. **3.** Because some nutrients, particularly vitamins, will have leached into the liquid. **4.** Because this shortens the cooking time and helps retain vitamin C.

Dry methods of cooking

Baking This involves placing food in a container – the food is cooked by the hot air which circulates in the oven. Although breads, cakes and pastries are baked, other healthier foods suitable for this method are poultry, lean meat, vegetables and fruit.

How it contributes to healthy eating	Link to health
Can be healthy if no additional fat is added, e.g. baked potato or apple filled with dried fruit, or if food, e.g. chicken, is cooked on a rack then the fat will drip off.	The reduction in fat lowers the risk of obesity, heart disease.
Nutrient loss is small.	Vitamins are retained which will contribute to general good health.

Grilling This involves cooking food under the direct heat of a grill, BBQ or grilling machine. Suitable foods are fish, thin good quality cuts of meat, chicken, vegetables.

How it contributes to healthy eating	Link to health
A very quick method of cooking which will save time and also retain the nutrients.	Vitamins are retained which will contribute to general good health.
Fat in food melts and drips out so grilling is a healthy method of cooking.	
No additional fat is required.	The reduction in fat lowers the risk of obesity, heart disease.
Lean or trimmed meat can be used so reducing the fat content.	

Pot roasting This involves cooking meat and poultry on a bed of vegetables in the oven where the food can be basted with fat if required.
Pot roasting should be carried out in a heavy pot or container with a tight-fitting lid. The pot roast can also be cooked on the hob over a gentle heat.

How it contributes to healthy eating	Link to health
Little or no fat is used.	The reduction in fat lowers the risk of obesity, heart disease.
There will be some nutrient loss but in some cases the cooking liquid is served as a gravy/ sauce.	Vitamins are retained which will contribute to general good health.
Vegetables are added and so contribute to healthy eating.	Vegetables will add fibre to the dish which prevents constipation and bowel disorders.

Roasting This is food cooked in the oven which is cooked by the hot air which circulates. Suitable foods include chicken, silverside, potatoes.

How it contributes to healthy eating	Link to health
If foods such as chicken, joints of meat are placed on a rack inside the roasting tin then the fat will drip from the food during cooking. No fat has to be added, particularly if the food is protected by tinfoil. Nutrient loss can be small.	The reduction in fat lowers the risk of obesity, heart disease. Vitamins are retained which will contribute to general good health.

Stir frying This involves cooking finely prepared foods such as vegetables, chicken, meat and fish in a small amount of oil for a very short time. Rice and noodles can also be stir fried.

How it contributes to healthy eating	Link to health
Only a small amount of oil or 'Fry Light' olive oil spray should be used. Using a non stick wok or frying pan will also cut fat content Vegetables are cooked quickly so most water soluble vitamins are retained. If large quantities of vegetables are used then this adds to the fibre content. Olive oil can be used to stir fry.	The reduction in fat lowers the risk of obesity, heart disease. Vitamins are retained which will contribute to general good health. Vegetables will add fibre to the dish which prevents constipation and bowel disorders. Olive oil is a monounsaturated fat which contains Omega 3 which is linked to reducing the risk of heart disease.

Shallow frying This involves cooking food in a small quantity of preheated oil in a shallow frying pan. Suitable foods are eggs, fish, poultry, thin cuts of good quality meat, vegetables.

Note: you will use this method of cooking in the unit called Practical Cookery Skills for the Hospitality Industry.

Top Tip You should not include this method in your NAB answers for this unit.

Microwaving This involves cooking food by the electromagnetic waves in a microwave oven. These waves penetrate the food from different directions, causing it to heat from the inside to the outside.

How it contributes to healthy eating	Link to health
Little or no fat is added. Food is cooked quickly so most nutrients are retained. Little water is used in cooking and so loss of water soluble vitamins is minimal. Salt does not require to be added to vegetables as the flavour is kept.	The reduction in fat lowers the risk of obesity, heart disease. Vitamins are retained which will contribute to general good health. The reduction in salt lowers the risk of high blood pressure, heart disease and strokes.

Planning your work

The key to success is effective planning and organisation of your practical work, whether in your kitchen at home, school or in a professional kitchen. Good planning ensures that all the dishes are prepared and cooked in the time you are allowed.

Effective planning will make you:

- confident
- prepared for work
- more aware of how to manage your time
- able to cope even when things go wrong
- enjoy what you are doing
- less stressed.

When planning your work there are a number of key terms that you need to be familiar with

- task – a piece of work to be undertaken or completed, i.e. a recipe
- component parts – the ingredients
- processes – the steps that have to be undertaken to complete the dish.

This unit will help you to build up your written planning skills as well as your time management skills, which will prepare you for the final SQA course award.

In this unit, Food Preparation for Healthy Eating, you have to provide a plan of work for **each** of the **three** dishes that you have amended to make healthier. You will be given opportunities to practise your planning skills before you are assessed, so let's look at the important points you must include in your plan of work.

Top Tip
During practical work keep a note of timings for different processes at the side of your recipes – this will be useful when planning.

Prepare a plan of work for the task

This means you have to:

Plan how you are going to carry out your task in a logical order in the time you have been given.

You need to consider the following:

Start time – 2 pm   Finish time – 3 pm

Top Tip
Remember to check the clock when starting to cook your dishes for any cookery process – timing is important to prevent either over or under cooking.

Plan what you are going to do within this time allocation.

'Think smart' and include the following areas in your plan of work:

- personal hygiene preparation – remove jewellery, put on clean apron, cover or tie back hair, wash hands
- collecting equipment
- collecting ingredients
- timings for the following activities:
  - preheating of oven
  - preparation of ingredients
  - cooking times
  - seasoning and tasting
  - testing for readiness
  - refrigeration if your dish has to be served cold
  - washing up – remember to 'clean as you go'
  - warming of serving dishes
  - presentation – garnishing and decoration
  - serving of the dish(es)

You will need to complete a work plan sheet similar to the one on the next page.

The purpose of the time plan is to allow you to plan and time the sequence of processes that you will have to complete when carrying out this task.

Quick Test

1. What personal hygiene preparations should be carried out before starting a practical task?

2. What is meant by 'processes'?

3. Why is 'clean as you go' important?

Answers: 1. Remove jewellery, put on clean apron, cover or tie back hair, wash hands. **2.** The steps that have to be undertaken to complete the dish. **3.** Stops dirty dishes building up.

Food Preparation for Healthy Eating

You need to complete a **plan of work**. It will look like this.

Times	Sequence of work	Notes
Times are normally allocated in blocks of 5 minutes – this will depend on the task. Try to divide your task into easily identified stages – these stages will combine a number of processes.	*Activities will include:* *– most of the activities listed on the previous page* *– all the stages of the recipe: preparation, cooking and serving* *– washing up*	*Notes could include:* *– oven temperatures* *– the finishing times of cookery processes* *– a reminder to place food in the refrigerator*

Here is a sample plan of work for **Curried Leek and Potato Soup** which has to be completed in 50 minutes from 10.00–10.50am

Ingredients

250 g leeks
100 g onion
300 g potato
15 ml oil
7.5 ml mild curry paste
800 ml vegetable stock
100 ml fat reduced single cream
Seasoning

Garnish
15 ml chopped parsley

Method

1. Collect all ingredients.
2. Prepare the following ingredients
   - Potato – wash, peel and finely chop.
   - Leek – wash and finely chop.
   - Onion – peel and finely chop.
   - Weigh all the prepared vegetables.
3. Heat the oil in a large pan and sauté the vegetables with the curry paste for 2–3 minutes or until they start to soften and colour.
4. Add the stock and bring to the boil. Reduce the heat, cover and simmer for 10 minutes or until all the vegetables are soft.
5. Chop the parsley.
6. Purée the soup in a food processor or blender until smooth. Taste the soup and adjust the seasoning if required.
7. Stir in the cream. Serve in a warm bowl sprinkled with chopped parsley.

Top Tip
Get into the habit of tasting your dish before serving – you will gain marks in the final practical assignment if your dish is well flavoured.

Times	Sequence of work	Notes
10.00–10.05 am	Personal hygiene, collect all the ingredients.	
10.05–10.15 am	Wash and prepare all the vegetables – finely chop onion, potato and leek. Weigh prepared vegetables.	
10.15–10.20 am	Heat the oil. Add the vegetables and the curry paste. Sauté the vegetables until starting to soften.	
10.20–10.30 am	Add the stock, boil and then simmer for approximately 10 minutes. Wash and chop the parsley. Wash the dishes and tidy unit.	Ready at 10.35 am approximately.
10.30–10.40 am	Collect and assemble food processor. Place serving dish to warm. Process soup until smooth. Taste soup.	
10.40–10.50 am	Stir in cream. Sprinkle with chopped parsley and serve. Complete all washing up and tidy unit. Finish.	

Quick Test

1. Complete a work plan for the recipe provided below. You have 50 minutes – from 10.10–11.00 am – to prepare, cook and serve the dish. Go to the **Learning Lab** for the proforma or draw your own similar to the one on page 52.

Spicy Mince with Rice
Ingredients
150g lean minced beef
100ml beef stock
75g onion
2 × 15ml spoons tomato ketchup
100g green pepper
150ml chopped tomatoes
5ml chilli powder
50g kidney beans
50g brown rice
5ml salt

Method
1. Collect ingredients.
2. Half fill a pan with cold water and salt and bring to the boil.
3. When the water boils, add the brown rice and simmer until tender. Drain when ready (approx. 20 mins).
4. Peel and chop the onion. Wash and dice pepper.
5. Place the mince and onion in a pan and dry fry until browned.
6. Add all the other ingredients. Bring to the boil and simmer 15 minutes, stirring occasionally.
7. Serve with the boiled rice.

Top Tip
Sometimes when planning your work you have to work backwards from the serving time. You may have to decide the latest possible time to start cooking the dish so that it is thoroughly cooked.

2. Explain what is meant by the term 'processes'.

3. What time block is suggested for tasks in your plan of work?

Answer

1.

Times	Sequence of work	Notes
10.10–10.15 am	Personal hygiene, collect all the ingredients. Put water on to boil for rice.	
10.15–10.20 am	Prepare onion and pepper. Add rice to water.	Test rice at 10.45 am
10.20–10.25 am	Dry fry mince and onion until brown.	
10.25–10.30 am	Add rest of the ingredients. Boil then simmer.	Ready approximately 10.45 am
10.30–10.40 am	Heat serving dish. Wash dishes. Tidy unit.	
10.40–10.45 am	Test rice. Drain. Place a border of rice on serving dish.	
10.45–10.50	Taste mince mixture then place into centre of rice. Serve.	
10.50–11.00 am	Wash all pans and unit tops. Wipe cooker. Finish.	

2. The steps that have to be undertaken to complete the dish.

3. Five minutes.

Costing of ingredients

For the hospitality industry, costing of ingredients is an important factor to consider when deciding on the overall price for dishes on the menu.

What should be considered before costing a recipe?

- Check how many portions the recipe is for – this means how many servings you will get from the recipe.
- To find out the cost of one portion you divide the total by the number of portions.
- Up-to-date prices can be obtained from most supermarkets' websites.

To get the price of 1 g of a solid ingredient or 1 ml of a liquid ingredient

Top Tip
Use a calculator.

– Divide the unit cost (how much the ingredient costs) by the unit weight or measurement (the weight or measurement the ingredient is sold in).

– This will give you the price of 1 g or 1 ml.

– Then multiply this by the weight or measurement of the ingredient required in the recipe.

Round prices **up** to the nearest pence if it is .5p or above, e.g. 12.5p would be rounded up to 13p.

Round prices **down** to the nearest pence if it is .49p or less, e.g. 12.4p would be rounded down to 12p.

Examples

If you were asked to price 50 g of butter, which costs 92p for 250 g:

Divide the unit cost of the butter by the weight of the butter, i.e. 92p divided by 250 g = .368p for 1 g of butter.
Multiply by the weight (50 g) required in the recipe = 18.4p.

Since the decimal place is less than .5, then it is rounded **down** to 18p.

If you were asked to price 75 ml of semi-skimmed milk, which costs 82p for 1000 ml:

Divide the unit cost of the semi-skimmed milk by the measurement of the semi-skimmed milk, i.e. 82p divided by 1000 ml = .082p for 1 ml of semi-skimmed milk.
Multiply by the measurement (75 ml) required in the recipe = 6.15p.

Since the decimal place is less than .5, then it is rounded **down** to 6p.

Now work out the cost of the following:

1. 300 g cooking apples at £1.45 for 1 kg
2. 75 g brown sugar at 79p for 500 g
3. 150 ml milk at 68p for 1 litre

Answers
1. 44p 2. 12p 3. 10p

For your assessment you will be asked to complete a costing exercise for a recipe which will be for four portions. You also have to work out the cost per portion so you will have to divide your total cost by four. An example is shown below for a Pasta Salad which serves four people.

Ingredients	Quantity	Unit cost	Cost £	p
Pasta shapes	120 g	£1.23 for 500 g		30
Red onion	100 g	43p for 500 g		9
Green pepper	125 g	£1.38 for 700 g		25
Cherry tomatoes	100 g	68p for 250 g		27
Light salad cream	150 g	£2.09 for 650 g		45
Edam cheese	50 g	£1.25 for 230 g		27
		Total cost	1	63
		Cost per portion		41

This is how this is worked out

Pasta shapes	Red onion
Unit cost £1.23 for 500 g	Unit cost 43p for 500 g
1 g costs £1.23/500 g = .002p	1 g costs 43p/500 g = .086p
120 g costs .002 × 120 = 30p	100 g costs .086 × 100 = 8.6p (round up to 9p)
Green peppers	**Cherry tomatoes**
Unit cost £1.38 for 700 g	Unit cost 68p for 250 g
1 g costs £1.38/700 g = .002p	1 g costs 68p/250 g = .272p
125 g costs. 002 × 125 = 25p	100 g costs =27p
Salad cream	**Edam cheese**
Unit cost £2.09 for 650 g	Unit cost £1.25 for 230 g
1 g costs £2.09/650 g = .003p	1 g costs £1.25/230 g = .005p
150 g costs .003 × 150 = 45p	50 g costs .005 × 50 = 27.1 (round down to 27p)

Quick Test

Look at the ingredients and costs of the ingredients used to make Carrot and Courgette Soup for four servings.

100 g onions at 72p for 1 kg

150 g carrots at 62p for 1 kg

200 g potatoes at 75p for 2.5 kg

200 g courgettes at 99p for 500 g

50 g lentils at £1.49 for 1 kg

1 chicken stock cube at 87p for 8

30 ml single cream at 40p for 150 ml

Copy the costing sheet below or visit the **Learning Lab** to download a blank copy.

Price the unit cost of each ingredient and then work out the cost of making one portion.

Ingredients	Quantity	Unit cost	Cost £	p
onions	100 g	72p for 1 kg		
etc.				

> **Top Tip**
> Visit the **Learning Lab** to complete your pricing using a spread sheet. If you were pricing large quantities of ingredients you would use this method.

Answers: Onions – 7p, carrots – 9p, potatoes – 6p, courgettes – 40p, lentils – 7p, chicken stock cube – 11p, single cream – 11p. Total cost – 8p. Cost per portion – 22p

Assessment practice

To help you pass the assessment for Food Preparation for Healthy Eating complete the following activities:

1. Read the following recipe for **Quiche Lorraine – 4 servings**

Ingredients

Shortcrust pastry
150 g plain flour
75 g margarine
6 × 15 ml water (chilled)

Filling

100 g streaky bacon
2 eggs
150 ml milk
75 g Cheddar cheese
Seasoning
15 ml chopped parsley

Method

1. Put on oven – 200° C, gas mark 6.
2. Collect all ingredients for the pastry.
3. Make the pastry.
4. Lightly flour the table and knead the pastry.
5. Roll out the pastry and line an 18 cm flan ring. Leave to relax for 5 minutes and then trim.
6. Bake blind for 10 minutes until set and pale golden in colour.
7. Prepare the following ingredients for the filling:
   - Bacon – cut into small pieces using kitchen scissors.
   - Cheese – grate.
   - Parsley – chop finely.
   - Beat together the eggs with the milk.
8. Scatter the bacon over the pastry base.
9. Pour the egg mixture into the flan and sprinkle with the cheese.
10. Bake for about 15 minutes until well risen and golden.
11. Sprinkle with the chopped parsley and serve.

   a. Adapt the ingredients to make the **Quiche Lorraine** healthier.
   b. Produce a plan of work for the altered recipe. The dish should be made in 55 minutes – from 10–10.55 am.

2. Using the food costing information provided below cost the recipe per portion.
   The **Savoury Mince with Rice** is for four portions.
   Download the proforma from the **Learning Lab**.

Ingredients	Per unit cost
300 g lean minced beef	£3. 90 for 500 g
150 g onion	72p for 1 kg
75 g tomato ketchup	80p for 250 g
200 g green pepper	£1.38 for 700 g
300 ml chopped tomatoes	34p for 400 ml
100 g kidney beans	33p for 400 g
150 g brown rice	78p for 500 g

3. a. List the wet methods of cookery.

    b. List the dry methods of cookery.

4. If you had to choose between frying and grilling a pork chop, which method would you choose and why?

5. Give three explanations on how stewing contributes to health.

6. By adding lentils to a stew, how will the nutritional content of the dish be improved and what effect will this have on health?

7. In poaching, the nutrient loss is minimised due to two factors. What are they?

8. Using the words provided in the word bank below, complete the information about steaming. Note there are extra words!

> Steam   Salt   Boiling   Heart disease   Vegetables   Indirect   Water   Fewer   Fish
> High blood pressure   Strokes   More   Overweight   Direct   Fat

In steaming food is cooked in the _____ rising from _____ water.

Suitable foods include _____ and _____. As the food does not

come into _____ contact with _____, _____ nutrients

are lost. Vegetables can be cooked without _____, which reduces the risk of

_____, heart disease and _____. As no _____ is required, this will

reduce the risk of _____.

9. Why should you place a joint of meat on a rack inside a roasting tin?

10. How can you cut fat content when stir frying?

11. Why should olive oil be use for stir frying?

12. Why is microwaving a good method to choose for cooking vegetables. Link your answers to the effect on your health.

Quick Test

Complete the following wordsearch about dry methods of cooking. All 16 answers can be found on pages 48–49.

V	I	T	A	M	I	N	S	O	B	T	M	K
A	B	E	T	W	C	O	T	P	D	V	I	C
G	O	V	E	R	W	E	I	G	H	T	Q	I
S	A	L	T	A	K	U	R	K	S	I	F	T
R	B	H	S	I	R	S	F	M	T	U	I	S
E	A	O	L	E	A	N	R	U	U	R	B	N
C	K	F	G	P	J	L	Y	D	N	F	R	O
H	E	A	R	T	D	I	S	E	A	S	E	N
I	D	T	I	J	E	X	L	I	F	A	H	A
O	U	A	L	H	O	P	K	J	X	U	E	Z
F	Y	I	L	E	V	A	W	O	R	C	I	M
D	E	N	I	A	T	E	R	W	A	E	R	P

What's this unit all about?

In this unit you will select a specific country to research. You will investigate the traditional foodstuffs and dishes of your chosen country. A range of dishes from your selected country will be produced.

There are two assessments for this unit.

1. **Written report**
   This covers Outcomes 1 and 2.

2. **Practical exercise**
   This covers Outcome 3.

Let's look more closely at what you have to do to be successful.

Outcomes you must complete

Outcome 1 – Identify a range of traditional foodstuffs used in one specific country

This means you have to:

- Correctly identify a range of traditional foodstuffs for the country you have chosen to investigate.
- Describe the characteristics of selected foodstuffs from the range you have chosen.

Outcome 2 – Investigate a range of traditional dishes produced in the specified country

This means you have to:

- Correctly identify a range of dishes for the country you have chosen.
- Describe the characteristics of the dishes you have selected.

Outcome 3 – Produce a range of traditional dishes from the specified country.

This means you have to:

- Produce the dishes you have selected to an acceptable edible standard.
- Ensure that the dish is traditional for the country you have selected.
- Produce the dish safely and in a hygienic manner.

India and **Italy** have been chosen to give you some guidance on the type of information you are expected to include in your report.

How to do well in your report

1. Select a country to research
   The country should be one for which you have access to a lot of information and resources. Make sure you have research information about your chosen country before you start. This could include background information on:

   - conditions which have influenced traditions such as climate, geography, culture, technology
   - cooking methods and traditional foodstuffs.

2. Complete the proforma from SQA using the following guidance.

Top Tip
Check the following guidance carefully to see that you have sufficient information to complete the report and that the foods are available to you before choosing your country.

Section 1

In this section you have to:

- Identify **two** examples of foods from your selected country for each of the following seven categories:
  Herbs and spices   Cereals and pulses   Meat and poultry   Fish
  Vegetables   Fruit   Dairy produce

Section 2

In this section you have to:

- Describe the characteristics of **five** traditional foodstuffs which you identified in Section 1.

You must choose each one from a different category.

For each one, you must use the following headings

- Origin (where the foodstuff originates)
- Production (how it is produced)
- Storage (how the foodstuff should be stored)
- Uses (how the foodstuff is used in cooking)
- Other varieties/types available

Section 3

In this section you have to:

- Identify **four** traditional dishes from the country you have selected.
  Each of the traditional dishes must come from a different category of the following:
  Cold dishes   Soups   Meat dishes   Fish dishes   Pasta dishes   Vegetable dishes
  Potato dishes   Salads   Sweets   Pastries   Breads

Section 4

In this section you have to:

- Research the characteristics of each of the **four** traditional dishes you selected in Section 3.

For each one, you must use the following headings

- A brief history of the dish
- The ingredients used
- The method – how the dish is made
- Variations of the dish

Introduction to India

Indian cookery is considered to be one of the most diverse cuisines in the world. Each region of India produces a wide range of distinctive dishes.

In the **northern** area of India, close to the Himalayas, the weather is temperate. Wheat is the main grain so plenty of bread is eaten here. Dishes are drier and can be scooped up using chapattis. Lamb, poultry, yoghurt, ghee and spices are used frequently. Food is often cooked in a clay oven called a tandoor.

To the **south** towards the equator, dishes become hotter. Rice is the main grain crop and a vegetarian lifestyle predominates. Fish, coconut, vegetables such as aubergines, okra, peppers and chillies are often used in cookery. More liquid curries are served in this area.

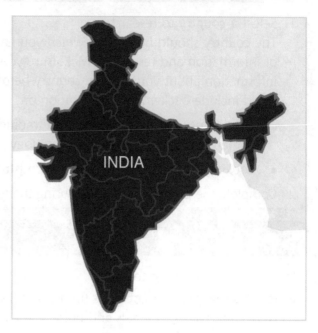

Along the **west** coast of India seafood dishes predominate. The Kerala coast is well known for its various fish curries and prawn dishes. Speciality dishes of this area include lamb or chicken with spiced lentils.

The region in the **east** has a plentiful supply of seafood from the Ganges Delta and the Bay of Bengal. A speciality dish of this area is a fish curry flavoured with yoghurt, turmeric and ginger.

The jungle areas of India offer mangoes, guava, bananas and coconuts.

Food customs are influenced by religion. The main religions are Hinduism, Islam and Sikhism.

Vegetarian cuisine is widespread, resulting from the predominance of Hindus. Strict Hindus believe it is wrong to kill animals so they do not eat meat, fish or eggs. Other Hindus do not eat beef since the cow is sacred to them, but they do eat lamb, poultry, fish and sometimes pork. Milk and milk products are used.

In contrast, Muslims rely on beef and lamb as an important part of their diet, provided they have been specially slaughtered and sold as halal meat from specific butchers. They do not eat pork.

Many Sikhs are vegetarians although they do not have any strict dietary guidelines.

In Indian cuisine, food is categorised into six tastes – sweet, sour, salty, spicy, bitter and astringent. A well-balanced Indian meal should contain all six tastes.

Despite regional variations, many of the foodstuffs are common throughout India. Let's look at some examples of these.

Top Tip
Look back at page 59 for a reminder of the background information you should research about your chosen country before you start.

Section 1: Range of Indian traditional foods

For your report Section 1 requires you to identify **two** examples of food for each of the seven categories below.

Here are some examples of each category for Indian cuisine.

Top Tip
Check you have identified a total of 14 different foods.

Foodstuff category	Examples
Herbs/spices	Bay leaves Turmeric Cumin Cardamom Fennel Nutmeg Sesame
Cereals/pulses	Lentils Chickpeas Mung beans Butter beans Red kidney beans Basmati rice Patna rice Flaked rice Semolina Vermicelli Flour Corn meal Gram flour
Meat/poultry	Lamb Beef Pork Chicken
Fish	Cod Shark Tuna Mackerel Prawns Crab Lobster Mussels
Vegetables	Okra Aubergine Onions Garlic Potatoes
Fruit	Apricots Coconut Sultanas Raisins Amla (Indian gooseberry) Mango
Dairy produce	Paneer Ghee Yoghurt Milk Cream.

Quick Test

Complete the crossword using the clues.

Clues

Across

1. A vegetable used in the south of India
4. Popular dishes in the west and east
7. Meat slaughtered in a special way
8. A type of dairy product
9. A white fish
10. A type of leaf

Down

2. A type of bean
3. A type of religion
5. A herb
6. A fruit

Answers: Across:
1. Aubergine 4. Seafood 7. Halal 8. Ghee 9. Cod 10. Bay.
Down:
2. Red Kidney 3. Islam 5. Fennel 6. Mango

Section 2: Characteristics of traditional foodstuffs

For your report Section 2 requires you to choose one **traditional foodstuff** from **any five categories** in Section 1.

Here are some examples of each foodstuff to show you the type of information you need to provide.

Top Tip
Remember you must be able to find enough information about origin, production, storage, uses and other varieties for each food. Choose your resources wisely.

Herbs and spices

Turmeric

Turmeric grows well in the tropical climate of India. The plant grows to a height of over 1 metre. Turmeric is the spice from the thick underground stem (rhizome) of the plant and needs temperatures between 20–30° C and considerable rainfall to grow successfully. The rhizomes are boiled for 45 minutes and then dried in hot ovens or the sun until they become hard and dry. They are then ground into a deep orange–yellow powder.

It is used as an ingredient in curry powder or on its own in fish curries, rice dishes, dhals and meat dishes. It is a preservative, so is used in pickles.

Turmeric can be bought fresh but is often bought dried and ground into powder form. An airtight container or spice jar should be used for storage. Use within four months or it will lose its vibrant colour. Saffron is another spice which will give a similar colour to dishes and is a member of the ginger family.

Cumin

Cumin is the seed of a small slender annual herb of the coriander family and can be grown extensively in India. The plant grows to 30–50 cm tall. Cumin seeds are the fruits of the herb. During drying of the seeds some fine stalks get left on, so cumin looks slightly bristly.

Cumin is a key component of chilli, curry and garam masala powders.

Cumin can be used to season many dishes made from meats, e.g. lamb and chicken, and is traditionally added to curries. Roasted cumin powder is sprinkled on top of salads or yoghurt as a dark contrasting garnish.

Cumin can be bought as seeds (used in breads and vegetable dishes) or in a powdered form – both require to be stored in airtight containers in a dry place away from light. The powder must be used within three months. Another variety is black cumin.

Cardamom

India is one of the major producers of cardamom. Cardamoms are the dried fruits of a herbaceous perennial of the ginger family which can grow 4–5 metres tall. The fruits or pods are picked just before they are ripe and then dried in the sun or drying houses. There are many different varieties of cardamom pods (such as lime green, brown) but they are all oval capsules

containing between 10–40 seeds. As soon as the seeds are crushed, the flavour and aroma are released.

Buy the whole seeds which can be ground in a mortar when needed. This ensures a rich flavour. Store the seeds in a clean, dry jar kept in a dark place. Indian savoury dishes such as rich red curries and rice dishes like biryanis use cardamom. Sweets dishes like milky desserts can be flavoured with cardamom. It is also used in garam masala.

Top Tip
Check out pages 75 and 76 for additional herbs and spices which also could be used in Indian cookery.

Cereals and pulses

Basmati rice

Top Tip
This rice should be washed and soaked before cooking and is the best rice to serve with Indian food.

This type of rice has been grown in paddy fields at the foot of the Himalayan mountain ranges in India for many years. Rice needs a hot climate and plenty of water so the paddy fields are kept flooded. Rice plants, which are thin, grow to about 1.5 metres.

When mature the plants are harvested, tied into sheaves and dried. Then they are threshed to separate the rice grains which are then cleaned and polished to give white rice.

Store in the packaging it comes in or in an airtight container for up to three months.

Basmati rice is available as a white rice and a brown rice. It can be an accompaniment for many dishes and can be made into biryanis, pulaos, sweets, stuffings and snacks. By adding some spices, nuts, dried fruits, vegetables, beans or meats to the rice a main meal can result.

Other varieties of rice include patna, ambemohar and red patni.

Bajra flour

This type of flour grows in India. When the bajra crop is ready to be harvested, the tall plants are cut, tied in and allowed to dry. The bundles are then threshed to separate the grains, which are then dried in the sun. This can then be processed into flour.

The flour should be stored in a dry jar. Bajra and jowar flours are often mixed to make bread or poppadoms. Other types of flours are wheat flour – wholemeal or white, jowar and gram flour.

Red lentils

Lentils are classed as pulses. Pulses are the edible seeds of certain plants. Red lentils are the seeds of a bushy plant which grows in cold climates and in non irrigated conditions throughout northern India, Madhya Pradesh and parts of Maharashtra. When ready, the long pods containing the lentils are plucked, dried and threshed. The lentils have a casing round them and are kept whole or peeled and split.

Lentils should be stored in a dry airtight container for six months. Lentils can be added to minced meat for kebabs, added to meat curries or seasoned with ginger and garlic.

Quick Test

1. What are lentils?

2. Describe the production of basmati rice.

3. How should cumin be stored?

4. What are the uses of turmeric?

Answers: 1. Pulse vegetable – the edible seeds of certain plants. **2.** Grown in flooded paddy fields, harvested when mature, tied into sheaves and dried. Then they are threshed to separate the rice grains which are then cleaned and polished to give white rice. **3.** Airtight container away from light. **4.** As an ingredient in curry powder, fish curries, rice dishes, dhals, meat dishes and pickles.

Meat and poultry

Lamb

A large proportion of Indian food is vegetarian but some traditional dishes include lamb. The meat from a sheep up to one year old is known as lamb, whereas the meat from an older sheep is known as mutton. In India the term mutton refers to goat meat and usually not to the meat from sheep.

Sheep and goats are raised primarily for their meat in India, as they are considered the most acceptable meat for Hindus, who eat meat occasionally. Beef is not eaten by most Hindus. Indian Muslims will eat lamb, mutton and goat but will not eat pork.

Slaughter often occurs at the household level, but some animals are purchased and brought to urban areas to be slaughtered. If the sheep is slaughtered according to halal, then the animal must be killed while conscious. As lamb is a high-risk food it should always be stored in the refrigerator at 4° C or less.

Indian cookery believes that to get the best from meat it should be cooked on the bone, as this will give it a more meaty flavour. Lamb can be used in many main dishes such as curries, tandoori dishes, meatballs, biryanis and spicy leg of lamb.

Fish

Prawns

India may not be thought of as a great fish eating nation but there are some parts of it, like Bengal, where fish and shellfish are very popular – tiger prawns being a favourite.

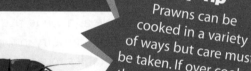

Top Tip
Prawns can be cooked in a variety of ways but care must be taken. If over cooked they develop a rubbery texture.

Prawns come in many different varieties and can be caught in back waters, estuaries and paddy fields as well as in the sea round India. The main method of prawn breeding is by using traditional farming methods in a hatchery. Post larvae stage prawns are acclimatised in nurseries and then transferred into grow out ponds where they are fed and grow until they reach marketable size.

Harvesting is done by either collecting the prawns after draining the pond or fishing the prawns out of the pond using nets.

As prawns are a food from which there is a high risk of food poisoning, they should always be stored in the refrigerator at 4° C or less.

Prawns can be used in curries, tandoori dishes, soups and pickles.

Other varieties are shrimps, crayfish, crab, mussels.

Vegetables

Okra

The okra is native to tropical Africa but also grows in India.

It is also known as lady's finger or gumbo. Okra seeds, which are quite large, will grow relatively quickly – in about 60 days. Large pale yellow flowers form but only bloom for one day and eventually form one okra pod. This pod should be picked when it is about 7 cm long. Because they contain seeds, they are technically fruit rather than vegetables but they are listed here with vegetables because of the way they are prepared and used in cooking. Okra is used in soup and dishes with rice. It appears in Indian cooking as bindi. Available fresh, canned or dried, it may be used to thicken soups and stews or simply eaten as a vegetable in its own right. Fresh okra should be stored in the refrigerator.

Onions

Onions are now grown all over the world.

Indian onions are white, pink or purple and can be small or large. They have a flattened stem at the base which increases in diameter as it grows. The leaves are long and hollow. The onion bulb grows underground and is formed by the thickening of the leaf base. The onions are dug up and left to dry until the skin hardens and becomes brittle.

Onions are frequently used in Indian cookery to give flavour, thicken or colour dishes. They are also used as garnishes, as an accompaniment, or sliced and served as a salad.

Onions are available in many forms – fresh, dried, powdered or flaked. Flakes and powdered onions are made by dehydrating fine slices of onions and should be stored in an airtight container. Fresh onions should be stored in a cool, dry place away from moisture.

Other varieties of the onion family are garlic, chives and spring onions.

Top Tip
Information on aubergines can be found on page 87 as part of the assessment practice. This vegetable is used in both Indian and Italian cookery.

Quick Test

Use the information found on pages 62–65 to help you find the 22 words in the wordsearch below.

G	A	R	L	I	C	H	K	E	B	A	B	S
N	Q	B	A	U	B	E	R	G	I	N	E	G
L	S	I	M	P	V	C	U	R	R	I	E	S
A	N	Y	B	T	U	E	A	F	Y	C	I	L
C	W	T	D	S	C	L	M	S	A	R	K	O
H	A	L	A	L	E	U	S	R	N	A	W	M
K	R	O	P	N	X	E	U	E	I	B	S	D
J	P	B	T	T	D	O	C	T	S	O	D	E
O	N	I	M	U	C	O	N	I	Q	G	O	C
F	L	A	K	E	D	F	O	L	R	O	P	I
S	K	V	E	G	E	T	A	R	I	A	N	L
R	E	T	H	G	U	A	L	S	I	T	B	S

Fruit

Apricots

Apricots grow in orchards on large leafy trees. In India the fruit ripen during the monsoon season when the weather is clement. The fruit is picked when ripe and dried in the sun or mechanically. In India the stone is left inside the apricot when dried.

Apricots are used in savoury dishes such as chicken, lamb and vegetable curries. They become plump as they absorb the cooking juices. They are used in desserts and are also served as part of an assortment of dried fruits after a meal.

Store dried apricots for up to six months in the refrigerator.

Coconut

The coconut is called the fruit of the Gods. The fruit is used in Hindu religious ceremonies. Coconut trees can grow up to a height of 20 metres. The fruit starts off being green and then matures to brown. Coconuts are picked when they are mature and left to dry until hard. The hard shell has to be broken to get to the coconut flesh.

Coconut is available fresh, desiccated, as milk or creamed. Creamed coconut is used as a base for curries. Grated coconut can be sprinkled on as a garnish. Desiccated coconut can also be used as garnishes, chutneys or desserts. It can also be used in curries where it is fried until golden brown and blended to a paste before being added. It can be used in a dessert as a stuffing between layers of pastry.

Fresh coconuts keep up to a week. The flesh can be grated and frozen for three months. Coconut milk or cream should be stored in a refrigerator.

Creamed coconut will keep up to six months in a refrigerator.

Top Tip
If you have made your curry too hot, use coconut milk to cool down the intensity of the flavour.

Sultanas/raisins

Indian grapes come in a variety of shapes and colours from green, orange, honey brown to purple black and are sun dried to increase their shelf life. The grapes, which will be dried to form sultanas and raisins, grow in orchards, hanging in bunches from vines. They are picked when mature as their sugar content is high and then laid out to dry in the sunshine. They are then graded, packed and distributed.

Raisins and sultanas should be stored at room temperature, in an airtight container, for about three months.

Raisins and sultanas are added to meat curries, biryanis, yoghurt-based accompaniments called raitas, chutneys, fruit salads and other desserts. They are also used in sweet pickles and in dishes made from paneer or cottage cheese.

Dairy produce

Paneer

This is a home made, unsalted white cheese similar to ricotta or cottage cheese. It has a dense crumbly texture that goes well with spices or served with flaky sea salt, freshly ground black pepper and a drizzle of olive oil. It is produced by boiling milk and then stirring in either yoghurt or lemon juice. Keep the milk on the heat, stirring gently to help the milk to curdle. The mixture will separate into curds and whey. The mixture should then be placed in a sieve which is lined with muslin and rinsed with cold water. The cheese should be wrapped in the muslin and allowed to drain for 10 minutes. Keeping the cheese still wrapped, a heavy weight should be placed on the top for 30–40 minutes until it is flattened into a firm block. It can then be cut. Keep the cheese in a water-filled, covered container in the refrigerator. It can also be frozen in an airtight container and defrosted before use. It can be used as an ingredient in wraps, on skewers for kebabs or vegetable dishes.

Ghee

Ghee is the purest form of butter fat. Ghee is clarified butter and is made from the milk of cows or buffalos. In India, buffalo milk is preferred due to its higher fat content, taste and colour. It is easily made from unsalted butter melted in a saucepan. The butter should be heated gently for about 30 minutes until all the water evaporates and the sediment settles and separates from the clear golden ghee. Cool the ghee slightly and strain into a metal or glass container. Cover and refrigerate once the ghee is completely cool. The ghee is now ready to use or it can be stored in the fridge. It is suitable for frying and sautéing ingredients when making curries. It is also used for desserts and for spreading on top of chappatis.

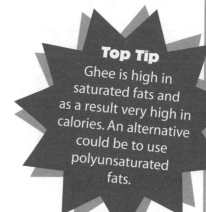

Top Tip
Ghee is high in saturated fats and as a result very high in calories. An alternative could be to use polyunsaturated fats.

Yoghurt

Yoghurt is made from curdled milk with the addition of a lactic starter.

Yoghurt becomes more sour tasting the longer it is stored. The yoghurt is used slightly sour for general cooking and very sour for specific dishes. Yoghurt should be fresh and sweet for desserts and raitas. The recipe will usually state whether it should be fresh or sour yoghurt. Yoghurt should be stored in a refrigerator. It can be added to savoury dishes such as curries and is also used as dressings for salads. Other varieties include bio and low fat yoghurts.

Quick Test

1. Explain how desiccated and creamed coconut are used in food preparation.
2. How is ghee produced?
3. How should sultanas be stored?
4. List some uses of apricots in food preparation.

Answers: 1. Desiccated coconut can be used for garnishes, chutneys or desserts. Creamed coconut can be used as a base for curries. **2.** The unsalted butter should be heated gently until the colour changes to pure gold. The impurities will have risen to the surface and should be removed with a spoon. The ghee is now ready to use. **3.** At room temperature and in an airtight container. **4.** In savoury dishes such as chicken, lamb and vegetable curries. They are used in desserts and are also served as part of an assortment of dried fruits after a meal.

Section 3: Traditional dishes of India

For your report Section 3 requires you to identify **one** example of a traditional dish from each of **four** categories below.

Here are some examples from each category for Indian cuisine.

Foodstuff category	Examples of traditional dishes
Starters	Vegetable and Cashew Samosas Garlic Mushroom Pakoras Onion Bhajias
Soups	Kanji (Thick Rice Soup) Rasam (South Indian Tamarind Soup) Subzion Ka Shorba (Spring Vegetable Soup)
Meat dishes	Tandoori Style Chicken Jardaloo Ma Gosht (Lamb with Apricots) Murgh Roghni (Chicken in Almond and Cashew Sauce)
Fish dishes	Prawn Bhuna Khatti Macchi (Baked Sour Fish) Goa Macchi (Goa Fish Curry)
Rice/pasta dishes	Gucchi Pulao (Mushroom Rice) Vegetable Pulao Sevian Kheer (Vermicelli Milk Pudding)
Vegetable dishes	Bharwan Tamater (Stuffed Tomatoes) Phoolgobi Rassa (Cauliflower in Coconut and Pepper Sauce) Tomatochi Kadhi (Tomato and Coconut Curry)
Potato-based dishes	Batata Talasani (Spicy Potato Straws) Banarasi Aloo (Potatoes in Sour Cream) Bombay Potatoes
Salads	Beet Raita (Sweet and Sour Beetroot Salad) Channe Ki Misal (Chickpea Salad) Aam Ka Sasam (Mango and Coconut Salad)
Sweets	Narial Ke Dosey (Sweet Coconut Pancakes) Alepak (Ginger Fudge) Satyanarayan Sheera (Rich Semolina Pudding)
Pastries	Karanji – dough using wheat flour, formed into pancakes, stuffed with a coconut, almond and raisin mixture and then fried in oil. Besan Ladoo – gram flour and ghee cooked together, cooled, sugar mixed in and formed into balls. Gulab Jamun – a dough which is formed into balls, fried and served with a sugar syrup.
Bread	Chapatti Naan Parathas

Top Tip
You will be making four of these dishes for your assessment in Outcome 3. Remember to choose ingredients that are available locally.

Section 4: Characteristics of traditional dishes

Dish 1 – PASTA – Sevian Kheer (Vermicelli Milk Pudding)

Brief history

It is not known how this Italian pasta became part of Indian cookery but it is likely that the name was borrowed and applied to a similar existing product in India. For Muslims the month of Ramadan is a holy month and people fast from sunrise to sunset. A traditional sweet to eat after sunset during Ramadan is made of fine vermicelli, milk, nuts and saffron.

Ingredients: Serves 4

60 ml ghee

10 ml cashew nuts

10 ml raisins

150 g vermicelli broken into pieces

300 ml milk

150 ml evaporated milk

75 ml caster sugar

Method

1. Heat the ghee carefully. Add the cashew nuts and raisins and fry until golden brown.

2. Add the vermicelli and fry gently until a light golden brown.

3. Add both types of milk and, stirring all the time, bring to the boil.

4. Simmer until the vermicelli is soft. Add the sugar and stir well.

5. Remove from the heat.

6. This dessert can be served hot or cold, garnished with additional nuts.

Top Tip

Other uses of vermicelli for Indian desserts include Sevian Sanja which includes ghee, raisins, flaked almonds, vermicelli, caster sugar and cardamom powder. The difference from the Sevian Kheer is that only a little water is used during cooking so this is a dry Indian dessert. Vermicelli is also used as an addition to clear soups, some stews and also as a snack.

Dish 2 – BREAD – Chapatti (or Roti)

Brief history

Wheat was ground into flour about 6000 years ago. Rough grinding stones have been excavated in India. In India people still buy whole wheat, clean it and take it to a mill to make sure that they get fresh pure flour. There are still a huge variety of breads eaten in India and these are usually cooked fresh for each meal. Chapatti is a basic wholewheat flat bread which is eaten with almost every meal in northern India. They are used to scoop up food and be dipped into sauces. In India chapattis are cooked on a tava or concave iron griddle, in the tandoor or clay oven, on an open fire or on earthenware pots.

Ingredients: Serves 4

450 g wholewheat flour (or half and half wholewheat and white plain flour)

10 ml sunflower oil

250–325 ml warm water as needed

Method

1. Sieve the flour into a baking bowl and add the sunflower oil. Mix with sufficient warm water to form pliable dough which is just slightly sticky.

2. Flour the table and knead for 8–10 minutes. You can, if you have time, place the dough into the bowl, cover with a damp tea towel and leave for 30 minutes in a slightly warm area.

3. Divide the dough into pieces the size of a golf ball. Flour the work surface and shape each piece into a ball.

4. Roll out each piece into a thin circle approximately 10–12.5 cm in diameter.

5. Heat a griddle or non stick frying pan until quite hot. A little oil can be added.

6. Ensure the heat is moderate and cook each chapatti until the surface becomes bubbly–about 1 minute.

7. Turn the chapatti over and cook the other side for about 1 minute until the base has small brown spots.

8. Traditionally the chapatti is held over an open flame to puff it up. As this can be dangerous, an alternative is to quickly heat the chapatti under a grill.

9. Serve immediately and keep warm by enclosing in a warm tea towel.

Top Tip
A similar dough can be used to make several other types of bread. Puris are small and round breads which are deep fat fried. Parathas are heavier layer breads which sometimes are stuffed with vegetables. Naan breads are raised by yeast and are baked in the oven.

Dish 3 – MEAT – Tandoori Style Chicken

Brief history

Tandoori Chicken is a chicken dish that originated in the Punjab region of India. The chicken is marinated in yoghurt and seasoned with tandoori masala. It is traditionally cooked at high temperatures in a clay oven (tandoor) but can be prepared on a traditional grill. One story of the origins of Tandoori Chicken is that in the 1920s a man called Kundan Lai Gujral ran a restaurant in Peshawar and decided to cook chicken in the tandoors used by locals to cook naan bread. The tandoors are bell shaped ovens, set into the earth and use wood or charcoal to reach temperatures of about 900 degrees. This allows the chicken to be crispy on the outside while the flesh is tender and cooked. Gujral moved his restaurant to Delhi, where his version of Tandoori Chicken found favour with the Prime Minister of India.

Ingredients: Serves 4

4 chicken breasts – wiped and skinned

200 ml natural yoghurt

10 ml chopped fresh root ginger

5 ml fresh garlic – crushed

5 ml chilli powder

10 ml ground cumin

2.5 ml black pepper

2.5 ml turmeric

10 ml ground coriander

5 ml ground nutmeg

2.5 ml red food colouring

To garnish: onion rings, lettuce, sliced lemon

Top Tip
Other variations include tandoori lamb, beef, monkfish or prawns. Tandoori powder is a ready-made mix of spices, red in colour, which can be added to curries.

Method

1. Make 2–3 slashes in each piece of chicken.

2. In a bowl place the yoghurt, ginger, garlic, chilli powder, ground cumin, black pepper, turmeric, ground coriander, ground nutmeg and red food colouring. Mix well.

3. Add the chicken to the bowl and mix well to coat. Cover and refrigerate for 3 hours.

4. Preheat the oven to 180° C or gas mark 4. Line a baking tray with foil.

5. Remove the chicken pieces from the marinade and place on the baking tray.

6. Bake for 45 minutes. From time to time baste with the remaining marinade.

7. Test the chicken pieces with the point of a knife. When juices run clear, then the chicken is ready.

Dish 4 – FISH –Prawn Bhuna

Brief history

The history of curry goes back a long way. It is likely that curry powder originated in India but its use is mentioned in a book written on English cooking in the late 1300s. The word 'curry' comes from 'Kari' which is from the Tamil language. Curry powder is not a single spice but a blend of different spices. In India, curry refers to a gravy or stew dish. These dishes contain the Indian spice mix of garam masala along with ginger, chilli, cumin, coriander, turmeric, onions and garlic. In India the curry ingredients will vary with the region. The spread of the popularity of curry to this country is attributed to the British Raj whose personnel acquired a liking for the spicy taste when stationed in India. They returned to this country and adapted the recipes to their own taste.

Ingredients: Serves 2

200 g cooked peeled prawns

1 clove of garlic – peeled and chopped

50 g onion – chopped

1 small fresh green chilli – washed, deseeded and cut into thin slices

10 ml garam masala

5 ml chilli powder

2.5 ml turmeric

15 ml sunflower oil

75 ml water

15 ml lemon juice

5 ml fresh coriander – washed and chopped

Method

1. Into a bowl place the chilli powder, chopped garlic, turmeric, garam masala and lemon juice.

2. Add the prawns and mix well. Leave to marinate in the refrigerator for 15 minutes.

3. Heat the oil in a pan and gently fry the onions on a low heat for 10 minutes until they are golden brown.

4. Add the prawn marinade and water. Cook for another 10 minutes until prawns are heated thoroughly and the water has evaporated.

5. Garnish the dish with the sliced chilli and chopped coriander.

Top Tip
Garam masala can be made from a mixture of up to 15 different spices. This can depend on the proportion of the different spices used and individual taste. Try to find out the spices which can be used.

Introduction to Italy

Italy is a boot shaped mountainous peninsula in southern Europe that extends into the Mediterranean Sea and has a population of around 58 million people. Several islands also form part of Italy; the largest are Sicily and Sardinia.

Being such a long narrow country the climate changes from snowy mountains in the very north, through the milder plains in the centre, to the hot dry lands in the south.

ITALY

Traditional Italian cooking has followed a very simple principle: food is best when it is cooked fresh and in season. Italians don't import a lot of produce – they cook what is grown locally. This goes a long way to explaining the diversity of Italian cuisine.

Wheat, rice and maize are grown in the north and there is good grazing land for cows and goats. These animals produce the milk for butter and cheese as well as being used for meat.

Olives grow in the warmer regions and are used for olive oil. Tomatoes and citrus fruits are also grown. Italy grows more of these fruits than any other European country.

In the southern state of Puglia on the 'heel' of Italy, the hard durum wheat used in the production of pasta is grown. The average Italian consumes 28 kg of pasta each year.

The seas around Italy provide a wide variety of fish including: sardines, tuna, anchovy, octopus and squid.

An Italian meal follows a strict pattern and consists of many courses. First, there are antipasti – an appetizer or soup. Then the first course, which is pasta, risotto or polenta. The second course is a meat or fish course – usually very small, served on its own. This is followed by the vegetable course or salad. To finish, there is cheese, then fruit or dessert.

As foods are mostly served on their own over a length of time, the individual flavours of foods and dishes can be so much more recognised and appreciated – Italian food is one of the great cuisines of the world.

Let's look at some examples of the range of Italian foodstuffs.

Quick Test

Use the information on this page to help you find the 16 words associated with Italy and Italian cookery.

M	O	H	S	I	C	I	L	Y	X	H	I
P	F	A	N	U	T	I	M	E	G	S	A
A	I	N	I	D	R	A	S	S	T	E	Y
D	N	O	S	A	E	S	L	J	B	R	V
N	A	L	A	L	U	P	T	Y	I	F	O
E	C	I	R	O	H	A	W	S	K	S	H
B	L	V	T	A	C	S	O	I	L	T	C
C	I	E	Y	S	F	T	G	U	Z	M	N
V	F	S	E	O	T	A	M	O	T	D	A
Q	E	T	O	O	B	H	D	I	U	Q	S

Top Tip
Look back at page 59 for a reminder of the background information you should research about your chosen country before you start.

Answers: Italy Sicily Sardinia Tuna Time Squid Fresh Season Olives Rice Tomatoes Pasta Anchovy Risotto Oil Boot

Section 1: Range of Italian traditional foods

For your report Section 1 requires you to identify **two** examples of food for each of the seven categories below.

Here are some examples of each category for Italian cuisine.

Foodstuff category	Examples
Herbs/spices	Saffron Basil Bay leaf Rosemary Oregano Marjoram Parsley
Cereals/pulses	Pasta – Tagliatelle, Spaghetti Rice – Arborio Polenta
Meat/poultry	Chicken Beef Pancetta Prosciutto Veal
Fish	Anchovy Tuna Prawns Shrimps Mussels Sardines
Vegetables	Aubergine Radicchio Capers Porcini mushrooms
Fruit	Tomatoes Olives Oranges Lemons Figs Grapes Pears
Dairy produce	Mozzarella cheese Parmesan cheese Ricotta cheese

Section 2: Characteristics of traditional foodstuffs

For your report Section 2 requires you to choose one **traditional foodstuff** from **any five categories** in Section 1.

Here are some examples of each foodstuff to show you the type of information you need to provide.

Top Tip
Use an Internet search engine to help you find information on Italian foodstuffs. Be quite precise when searching for your information, e.g. history of Italian herbs.

Herbs and spices

Rosemary

Rosemary is the most commonly used herb in Italy. Its leaves are spiky, green–grey in colour with an aromatic, pine like flavour with a hint of lemon. It can grow wild in many areas of Italy.

If at all possible, grow your own. It does particularly well against a sunny wall, giving violet blue flowers twice a year. For culinary use, snip off the tips of the younger, more fragrant branches.

Cook only with fresh cut rosemary or, if you have to store, the salad drawer of the refrigerator will keep it fresh till required.

In Italy rosemary is usually associated with roasts, giving full flavour to chicken or rabbit. It is particularly good with pan roasted potatoes, some fragrant pasta sauces, in frittatas and in various breads.

Rosemary can be used dried (whole leaves); chop some and then crumble the rest to release the flavour. Use about half the quantity you would need if they were fresh.

Saffron

This comes from the orange coloured stigmas of a mauve flowering crocus. It is a native of southern Europe. It is an expensive spice because the stigmas have to be picked by hand and over 200,000 of them are required to make 500 g of saffron. However, only a small quantity is needed in cookery.

Saffron powder should be stored carefully in an airtight container in a dry place, away from light.

It is aromatic, pungent and slightly bitter and it has a brilliant yellow dye. It enhances Italian fish, chicken and rice dishes, e.g. Risotto with Saffron (Milanese style).

It is available as stigmas or powder.

Quick Test

1. Name two Italian cheeses.

2. Name two types of Italian pasta.

3. Explain how you would use dried rosemary.

4. Why is saffron expensive?

Answers: 1. Mozzarella, Parmesan or Ricotta cheese. **2.** Tagliatelle or spaghetti – or any other type acceptable. **3.** Use whole leaves of rosemary; chop some, and then crumble the rest to release the flavour. Only use half the quantity you would need for fresh. **4.** It is hand picked and over 200,000 stigmas are required to make 500 g of saffron.

Foods of the World

Bay leaves

Although originally a native of India, bay grows well in warm tropical climates.

This evergreen tree grows to a height of 8 metres. The leaves are ready for harvesting when the trees are 10 years old. Small branches with leaves are dried for 3–4 days, then tied into bunches before being sold at markets. Sometimes the leaves are separated and packed into bamboo nets.

These leaves are used in meat and rice dishes and are removed before serving. They are added to hot oil at the beginning of cooking as frying releases their sweet woody aroma, similar to cinnamon. In India they are part of garam masala.

Bay leaves are sold dried and can be stored in an airtight container for six months.

Basil

There are many varieties of basil and it is sweet basil which is prominently featured in Italian cuisine. It has a strong, sweet flavour and can smell grassy and hay like.

Basil thrives in a sunny spot outdoors but it can be grown indoors in a pot on a sunny windowsill and will need regular watering. Basil can be propagated from cuttings kept in water until roots develop. If a basil plant is allowed to flower, it may produce seed pods containing black seeds which can be saved and planted.

The fresh herb can be kept for a short time in a plastic bag in the refrigerator or for a longer time in the freezer after blanching. The dried herb loses its flavour quickly and weakens significantly.

Basil is one of the main ingredients in pesto – a green Italian oil and herb sauce from the city of Genoa.

It is recommended that basil is always used fresh and in cooked recipes it is generally added at the last moment as to maintain flavour and appearance.

Lemon basil has a strong lemony smell and flavour. It is very different from other varieties and can be used in salads.

Cereals and pulses

Rice – Arborio

As Europe's leading rice producer, Italy specialises in varieties of short ovular grains grown for the cooking of risotto. Arborio rice is Italian medium grain rice. It is named after the town of Arborio in the Po Valley where it is grown.

The high starch kernels are shorter and plumper than any other. It partly dissolves to become clingy and creamy in texture but at the same time be firm to the bite.

Rice should be transferred from the packet to an airtight container (add a few bay leaves) and kept in a cool dry place. Take a note of the 'best before' date on the packet before storing.

There are many risotto recipes, e.g. Milanese Risotto, showing the wide variations of local Italian cuisine.

Italy produces several varieties of rice for risotto other than arborio. Vialone, nano and camaroli are also used.

Top Tip

Italians recommend that the perfect risotto is made by not adding too much liquid at once; not adding any additional liquid until the previous addition has been absorbed; and stir, stir, stir!

Pasta

It is known that the Romans ate pasta, as ancient pasta making equipment is exhibited in Pompeii Museum. The word 'pasta' simply means 'dough' and is the staple diet of Italy.

There are two main types: the factory-made flour and water paste, called 'pasta secca' (dry pasta as sold in packages) and the fresh pasta made with flour and eggs, called 'pasta all'nova' (home made pasta). The dough for factory pasta is composed of semolina (hard wheat) and water. The shapes the dough is made into are obtained by extruding the dough through perforated dies (small holes). Once shaped the pasta must be fully dried before being packaged.

The basic dough for home made pasta consists of egg and soft wheat flour. It is then rolled out by hand or a hand-cranked machine and then shaped by hand. One is not better than the other – simply different.

The storage time for pasta varies from days to years depending on whether the pasta is made with egg or not, and whether it is dried or fresh. Pasta is boiled 'al dente' (not too soft) prior to eating.

There are approximately 350 different pasta shapes.

Quick Test

1. Describe Italy's risotto rice.
2. How should rice be stored?
3. Name the two main types of pasta which are produced.
4. How should pasta be cooked?

Answers: 1. The high starch kernels of this Italian grown grain are short and plump. It partly dissolves to become clingy and creamy in texture but at the same time be firm to the bite. **2.** In an airtight container and kept in a cool dry place (add a few bay leaves). **3.** Dried or fresh. **4.** Pasta is boiled to 'al dente' (not too soft).

Meat and poultry

Prosciutto de Parma (Parma ham)

One of the earliest references to ham production in Parma appeared about 100 BC. It was the process of burying pork legs in barrels filled with salt. The meat was then dried and smoked. As the process of making air-cured Parma ham was refined, the smoking step was discontinued.

Top Tip
Salt is used to cure many Italian meats and fish – which can give very strong salty flavours. This can spoil the flavour of the food.

Prosciutto is a hog's hind thigh or ham which has been salted and air dried. Salt draws off the meat's excess moisture. Depending on the size of the ham, the curing process may take from a few weeks to a year or more. Slow, unforced, wholly natural air curing produces the delicate, complex aromas and sweet flavour that distinguish the finest prosciuttos.

Sliced prosciutto should be eaten as soon as possible or it will quickly lose its flavour. If it must be kept for a length of time, each slice or each single layer of slices must be covered with cling film and then tightly wrapped in tin foil. Plan on using it within 24 hours but remove it from the refrigerator one hour before serving.

Prosciutto contributes a huskier flavour to pasta sauces, vegetables and meat dishes than any other ham. It can often be served as antipasto, wrapped around melon.
Culatella is a special variety of prosciutto, which is aged and may be cured with wine.

Fish

Anchovy

The anchovy is a dark blue and silver fish found in the Mediterranean off the coast of Italy. It is usually about 4–8 cm, but can grow to 20 cm. The fresh fish is excellent, with white flesh and a good flavour, but nothing like the flavour of the anchovy when cured. This art has been known to the peoples of the Mediterranean for thousands of years.

Curing develops the flavour and colour only after the anchovy has been pickled in salt for some months and fermentation results. Plain salted anchovies should be soaked in water for a short time to remove some of their salt before being used. Anchovies can also be canned in oil but are very strong tasting and the flavour can play a dominant part in the dish. A jar of salted anchovies will keep almost indefinitely.

Italy has a sauce called 'bagna cauda', which consists of anchovies melted in a mixture of oil and butter. This is eaten with vegetables as a dip. Pizzas are often garnished with anchovies. Anchovies are regarded more as flavouring than a major ingredient.

They are available salted in jars or canned in oil.

Vegetables

Radicchio

This crisp red leafed member of the chicory family is from the Treviso area of northern Italy. The leaves are firm and crisp with a slightly bitter, peppery taste. Radicchio is easy to grow, particularly in spring. It prefers frequent watering depending on soil. Infrequent watering will make it bitter. Radicchio matures about three months into its growing cycle. It can be grown all year round.

Radicchio stores well in storage conditions of 3–5° C for two weeks.

Its rich dark red colour makes it a dramatic addition to mixed salads and an excellent garnish. It can also be used in soups, sauces and as braised vegetables.

Radicchio Chioggia is the most widely available variety. Another variety similar in shape, but with slightly looser leaves of mottled pink is called Radicchio di' Castelfranco.

Fruit

Tomatoes (Pomodori)

The tomato is the fruit of a plant which is a member of the deadly nightshade family. Tomatoes are native to South America and the seeds were brought back to Europe in 1519. Italy was the first to cultivate the tomato outside South America.

Tomatoes are grown for their flesh. Both the water and seeds in the middle and the skin have absolutely nothing to contribute to the flavour of the fruit. In Italy there are many types which come in a variety of colours, shapes and sizes. The most flavoured are those ripened on the vine. Choose firm tomatoes, richly coloured and fragrant.

Ripe tomatoes should be stored at room temperature and used within a few days. Never refrigerate tomatoes as the cold temperature kills the flavour and turns the flesh grainy.

Tomatoes can be bought fresh, tinned or sundried and are eaten raw or cooked. Red tomatoes are available also as juice, purée or ketchup. Tomatoes can form part of many classic Italian recipes, e.g. Parma and Tomato Pizza, Baked Stuffed Tomatoes with Lemon, Basil and Parmesan Rice and Bolognese Sauce.

Top Tip
Cooked tomatoes will give a good supply of antioxidants which helps prevent certain cancers.

Quick Test

Complete the crossword using the information on pages 78–79.

Across

1. The Italian name for ham

5. The name for the first course of a meal

6. A small fish

Down

1. Where ham is produced

2. People sometimes class this as a vegetable

3. Anchovies can be canned in this

4. A popular Italian dish

Answers: Across 1. Prosciutto **5.** Antipasti **6.** Anchovy. **Down: 1.** Parma **2.** Tomato **3.** Oil **4.** Pizza

Dairy produce

Top Tip
A pizza can incorporate so many Italian foodstuffs. Think of the wide variety of cheese, vegetables, fruit, meat, fish, herbs which you could experiment with when making your own pizza.

Parmesan (Parmigiano)

The name of this cheese is strictly protected by law as it is produced by a process unchanged in seven centuries. It comes from the partly skimmed milk of cows raised in the provinces of Parma and Reggio Emilea.

It is produced by a totally natural process – nothing is added to the milk but rennet and a long ageing process of at least two years. It is said that the pastureland of this area contributes to its distinctive taste. This hard cheese has a grainy texture and a rich nutty flavour.

This cheese is best stored by wrapping it tightly in greaseproof paper, then in tinfoil, to prevent it from drying out and kept on the bottom shelf of the refrigerator.

Grated or shaved parmesan cheese is widely used in typical Italian recipes such as Minestrone, pasta dishes or in sauces.

Blocks of fresh parmesan are available from good delicatessens and can be categorised by age, e.g. old, extra old, four or five years old or less mature. Tubs of grated parmesan are widely available from supermarkets.

Mozzarella

At one time, all mozzarella was made from water buffalo milk. The buffaloes graze on the pastures of Campania, the southern region of which Naples is the capital. Now it is usually obtained from cow's milk.

The buffalo milk is much creamier than cow's milk, and the cheese it produces is white and velvety in texture, pleasantly fragrant and sweet but delicately savoury.

It is made using 'spinning and then cutting' (hence the name: the Italian verb mozzare means 'to cut'). It is a semi-soft cheese. Due to its high moisture content, it is traditionally served the day it is made but can be kept in brine for up to a week or longer if sold in vacuum sealed packages.

Pizza, when it was created in Naples, was always made with mozzarella di bufala. It is used in lasagne and is served sliced, with sliced ripe tomatoes and basil, in the salad 'Insalata Caprese'.

It is made in various shapes, such as rounds, slabs or shredded.

Section 3: Traditional dishes of Italy

For your report Section 3 requires you to identify **one** example of a traditional dish from each of **four** categories below.

Here are some examples from each category for Italian cuisine.

Top Tip
You will be making four of these dishes for your assessment in Outcome 3. Remember to choose dishes that are within your skill level.

Foodstuff category	Examples of traditional dishes
Starters	Mozzarella e Pomodori (Mozzarella and Tomatoes) Aubergine Salad Crostini Alla Fiorentina (Paté on Crusty Fried Bread)
Soups	Minestrone Pasta and Bean Soup Zuppa di Pesce (Fish Soup)
Meat dishes	Chicken Cacciatora Arrosta di Maiale (Roast Pork Italian Style) Ossobuco (Stewed Shin of Veal)
Fish dishes	Baked Fillet of Sole with Tomato, Oregano and Hot Pepper Pan roasted Mackerel with Rosemary and Garlic Sea bass with Fennel, Sicilian Style
Rice/pasta dishes	Milanese Risotto Lasagne Tortellini
Vegetable dishes	Broccoli al Prosciutto (with ham) Fagiolini in Umido (French Beans with Tomato and Basil) Melanzane e Pomodori al Forno (Gratin of Aubergines and Tomato)
Potato-based dishes	Gnocchi al Pesto Potato and Ham Croquettes, Romagna Style Mashed Potatoes Bolognese Style (with milk and parmesan)
Salads	Cannellini Bean Salad Italian Potato Salad Radicchio and Warm Bean Salad
Sweets	Zabaglione Ricotta Ice Cream Tiramisu
Pastries	Pear Tart Chiacchiere (Golden Slices) Tortine di Cioccolato (Chocolate Tarts)
Bread	Focaccia Ciabatta Olive Oil Bread

Quick Test

Use the information on pages 80–81 to complete the wordsearch.

M	O	Z	Z	A	R	E	L	L	A	E	P
S	I	G	N	O	C	C	H	I	T	N	R
E	L	N	V	O	F	C	U	K	S	O	O
V	D	S	E	A	B	A	S	S	A	I	S
I	N	Q	W	S	M	I	B	Y	P	L	C
L	R	I	C	O	T	T	A	L	S	G	I
O	T	T	O	S	I	R	H	U	T	A	U
O	S	S	O	B	U	C	O	H	R	B	T
K	F	O	L	A	S	A	G	N	E	A	T
R	A	D	I	C	C	H	I	O	E	Z	O

Section 4: Characteristics of traditional dishes

Dish 1 – SOUPS – Minestrone

Brief history

Minestrone is the name for a variety of thick Italian soup made with vegetables, often with the addition of pasta or rice. It was a very humble dish and was intended for everyday consumption, being filling and cheap, and would likely have been the main course of a meal. Minestrone is part of what is known in Italy as 'Cucina Pouera' meaning poorer people's cuisine.

Due to its unique origins in the 1600s and the absence of a fixed recipe, Minestrone has many variations across Italy. The introduction of new ingredients from the Americas in the middle ages, including tomatoes and potatoes, also changed the soup to the point that tomatoes are now considered a staple ingredient, though the quantity used varies from northern to southern Italy.

Ingredients: Serves 4

½ onion, peeled and diced

1 carrot – washed, peeled and diced

1 stalk celery – washed and thinly sliced

50 g cabbage – washed and shredded finely

50 g frozen peas

1 clove garlic, peeled and crushed

2 rashers of bacon or pancetta, fat removed and cut into even sized pieces

15 ml olive oil

1000 ml water

450 ml tinned Italian tomatoes

1 vegetable stock cube

pinch salt, pepper and oregano

50 g pasta shapes or spaghetti broken into 2 cm pieces

To serve: 50 g grated parmesan cheese

Top Tip

Minestrone varies depending on the traditional cooking times, ingredients and season. Minestrone ranges from a thick and dense texture with very boiled down vegetables which will have been cooked for a long time, to a more broth like soup with large quantities of diced and lightly cooked vegetables that may include meats.

Method

1. Prepare all the ingredients.
2. Heat the oil gently, sauté the onions for 2 minutes, add bacon and garlic and sauté another 2 minutes.
3. Add carrot, celery and sauté again for another 2 minutes without colouring.
4. Add the tomatoes and stock to the pot, bring to the boil and simmer for 30 minutes.
5. Add cabbage and pasta wand cook for 10 minutes.
6. Add peas and cook for a further 5 minutes.
7. Taste the soup and adjust the seasoning if required.
8. To serve, ladle soup into bowls and sprinkle with parmesan cheese.

Dish 2 – MEAT – Chicken Cacciatora

Brief history

Cacciatore means 'hunter's style'. This dish developed in central Italy and has many variations. It is considered a country style dish in which chicken pieces are simmered together with tomatoes and a variety of vegetables. The dish originated in the Renaissance period (1450–1600) when only the well-to-do could afford to enjoy poultry and the sport of hunting.

Ingredients: Serves 4

200–250 g chicken – wiped and cut into bite size pieces

15 ml olive oil

25 g plain flour (spread on a plate)

salt and freshly ground black pepper

1 onion, very thinly sliced

1 sweet yellow or red pepper – washed and cut into julienne strips

1 carrot – washed and cut into thin slices

½ stalk celery – washed and thinly sliced

1 clove garlic – peeled and finely chopped

150 g tinned chopped Italian plum tomatoes and juice

150 ml chicken stock

Top Tip

The range of vegetables used can be seasonal and a bunch of fresh herbs can also be added, e.g. sprigs of fresh parsley, bay leaves, rosemary and celery leaves could be tied together and added to the pot to give added flavour.

Method

1. Coat the chicken pieces in the flour. Heat the oil and brown the chicken. Transfer to a warm plate and season with salt and pepper.

2. Add the onion to the pan and cook until golden. Return chicken to the pan and add pepper, carrot, celery, garlic and chopped tomatoes and juice.

3. Adjust heat to cook at a slow simmer and cover.

4. Cook until chicken is tender and thoroughly cooked (not pink). If sauce is thin, remove chicken pieces and reduce sauce over a high heat.

5. Pour contents of pan over the chicken and serve at once.

Variations of dish

There are many variations in the dishes that go by the cacciatore name, but they generally consist of chicken or rabbit fricassée with tomato, onion and other vegetables.

Dish 3 – PASTA – Lasagne

Brief history

Although the dish is generally believed to have originated in Italy, the word 'lasagne' is thought to derive from the Greek word meaning 'trivet' or stand for a pot. The Italians then borrowed the word to mean cooking pot. Another theory suggests that it comes from the Greek word 'lasanum', which means a kind of flat sheet of pastry dough cut into strips.

Lasagne is both a form of pasta in sheets and also a dish, sometimes named 'Lasagne al forno' (meaning 'oven-cooked lasagne') made with alternate layers of pasta, cheese, and often ragu (a meat sauce) or tomato sauce.

Ingredients

100 g 'no cook' lasagne sheets

Meat Sauce
1 small onion
1 × 15 ml spoon oil
150 g mince
1 × 10 ml spoon flour
pinch of mixed herbs and dried oregano
100 g chopped tomatoes
1 × 15 ml spoon tomato purée
Salt and pepper
1 clove of garlic, crushed
125 ml stock

Cheese Sauce

25 g margarine
25 g flour
250 ml milk
salt and pepper
50 g grated parmesan or strong cheese

Method

1. Peel and chop the onion and fry in the oil until soft. Add garlic.

2. Add mince and stir until browned. Add flour.

3. Add remaining meat sauce ingredients.

4. Bring to the boil, stir then reduce the heat until simmering.

5. Simmer for 30 minutes, adding more stock if it begins to dry up.

Cheese Sauce

6. Melt margarine in pan, add flour and mix well.

7. Remove from heat and gradually add milk, stirring well.

8. Return pan to heat and stirring continuously, allow the mixture to boil.

9. Stir in the cheese.

10. Place half the cooked mince in your dish. Add a layer of lasagne sheets, then half the cheese sauce.

11. Repeat this process once.

12. Bake in the oven for 30–40 minutes at 180° C, gas mark 4.

Top Tip
Another variation is Lasagne Verde (green lasagne) which is normal egg pasta with spinach added. Other variations include vegetarian or seafood versions of the dish. Using the 'no cook' lasagne sheets will save you time.

Variations of dish

Various recipes call for several kinds of cheese, most often ricotta and mozzarella. The classic Lasagne alla Bolognese uses only Parmigiano Reggiano. Many recipes also add bechamel sauce.

Dish 4 – SWEET – Tiramisu

Brief history

During the 17th century a similar dessert was created in Siena, in the north-western Italian province of Tuscany. The occasion was a visit by Grand Duke Cosimo de Medici (1642–1723). He brought the recipe back with him to Florence. In the 19th century, tiramisu became extremely popular among the English intellectuals and artists who lived in Florence. The name Tiramisu is from the Italian and means 'pick me up' but can be translated figuratively as 'make me less sad/happier'.

Ingredients

2 eggs

20 ml caster sugar

10 sponge fingers

50 ml strong coffee

20 ml brandy (or 10 ml brandy essence)

5 ml cocoa powder

100 g mascarpone cheese

Top Tip
Remember this recipe is a classic Italian sweet but does contain raw eggs which can be a source of bacteria. The food industry often uses pasteurised egg white in recipes like this.

Method

1. Place sponge fingers in the bottom of a shallow dish.

2. Sprinkle the sponge fingers with the coffee and brandy essence. Leave to soak.

3. Separate the eggs.

4. Whisk the egg whites until stiff.

5. Beat the egg yolks, sugar and mascarpone cheese until smooth.

6. Fold the egg white into the mascarpone mixture.

7. Pour the mixture evenly over the sponge fingers.

8. Sprinkle lightly with cocoa powder and place in refrigerator.

Variations of dish

In the original recipe, there was no alcohol as the cake was originally made for children and the elderly. The original shape was round. The ingredients used were finger biscuits, eggs, sugar and cocoa.

Assessment practice

To help you pass the assessment for Foods of the World complete the following activities:

1. Read the following information on **aubergines.**

The aubergine, also known as eggplant, is a member of the deadly nightshade family. It bears a fruit which is commonly used as a vegetable in cooking. It originated in tropical Asia and is commonly grown in India. In tropical climates the eggplant is sown directly into the soil. It can grow from 40–150 cm tall and has large leaves that are 10–20 cm long and 5–10 cm wide. The stem is often spiny. The fruit are cut from the vine.

Aubergines can grow in several shapes – they may be long, oval, or round, and they vary in colour from white to green to purple. They are used in many Indian/Italian dishes to add flavour and colour.

Aubergines may be sliced and boiled, fried, or added to curries, chutneys, stuffed with meat and rice and then baked. Aubergines can have a bitter flavour and are usually salted before use to remove the bitter juices.

They should be stored in the salad drawer of the refrigerator.

Answer the following questions:

a. Where did aubergines originate?

b. How are they stored?

c. How are aubergines used in cookery?

d. What varieties of aubergine are available?

e. Describe how they are produced

2. To help you develop your **research skills** further, try the following activities. Use Internet websites to find the following information:

Find out the **history** and **varieties** of **each** of the following dishes:
a. Italy: Neapolitan Pizza   b. India: Samosas

For the following vegetable – Garlic – find out:
Origin, Production, Storage, Uses, Varieties

For the following herb – Parsley – find out:
Origin, Production, Storage, Uses, Varieties

3. To help you with your practical work for Foods of the World, complete the following:

Explain why each of the following points is important for good personal hygiene when handling food.

Nail polish must be removed   No jewellery should be worn   No smoking in the kitchen

Teacher or supervisor must be informed if the food handler is suffering from diarrhoea

4. Look back at the following recipes:
a. Prawn Bhuna on page 72
b. Chicken Cacciatora on page 83
c. Tiramisu on page 85

For **each dish,** list the main points to be observed to ensure food is hygienically and safely prepared.

How to do well in your practical assignment

To achieve the SQA Course award you will have to plan and complete a practical assignment. In the assignment you will use all the skills – planning, preparation, cooking and serving – that you have learned during the completion of the three units of the Hospitality: Practical Cookery Intermediate 2 course.

The practical assignment for the Hospitality: Practical Cookery Intermediate 2 course is worth 100 marks and consists of two parts:

- Planning – 15 marks
- Preparing, cooking and serving food – 85 marks

Three dishes – a starter, main course and a dessert – have to be prepared in 2½ hours. Each dish is for four portions.

Planning and preparation

All your planning will be completed in a Planning booklet which is issued by the SQA.

Plan of work

In this booklet you have to complete a plan of work. It will show how you intend to use the 2½ hours on the day of your practical assignment to complete the three dishes issued by SQA.

You also have to describe the service details of all three dishes. Look at the example given below.

Service details for **Individual White Chocolate Cheesecake**

Four clean, white, cold tea plates. A labelled diagram could also be included to indicate the fruit coulis a few fresh raspberries lying beside the cheesecake.

Preparation time

Before you start to plan, there are certain preparations you are allowed to do during preparation time – this is usually ½ hour before you start your practical assignment.

The preparation time is important to allow you to be organised and calm before you start.

Remember: these preparations should not be included in your plan of work.

What are you allowed to prepare before the start of the practical assignment?

'Set up' your own personal work area with all the equipment needed for preparing, cooking and serving the foods.

Preheat the oven during preparation time but you must turn it off before you start the practical assignment.

Weighing and measuring can be done in advance but preparation of raw ingredients is not allowed, e.g. peeling of vegetables.

Top Tip

You are allowed to practise each of your dishes once in school. You should do this before you do your plan of work as you can make notes on the recipe to show how long you took for each stage of the recipe. This will give you a rough idea of how long you will take to do each activity.

How to do well in your practical assignment

If you want to prepare any extra garnishes or decorations you can do this in the preparation time unless the recipe states 'prepare garnish'.

Where an ingredient states 'finely chopped parsley' this can be prepared during your preparation time.

Fresh herbs can have leaves picked from the stalk.

Starting your plan of work

You will be awarded the full 8 marks if your plan is in a logical order and you have managed to do this on your own.

It must show the sequence in which you are going to carry out all the activities involved in the production of the three dishes.

Use the following list to ensure your plan of work contains all the required information.

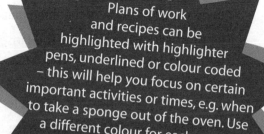

Top Tip

Plans of work and recipes can be highlighted with highlighter pens, underlined or colour coded – this will help you focus on certain important activities or times, e.g. when to take a sponge out of the oven. Use a different colour for each course – starter, main course or sweet – as this makes it even clearer.

Plan of work

- Indicate the start and finish times clearly.
- Allow a few minutes at the beginning of the plan to carry out personal hygiene preparations.
- Include turning on the oven and switching off when finished.
- Include temperature of oven.
- It is easier to plan if you break the timings of your activities into 5, 10 or 15 minute blocks.
- Check you have allowed enough time for various activities, e.g. vegetable preparation, browning of meat.
- Check the cooking time of each dish and allow the correct length of time.
- Check the serving times of your dishes. You may have to work backwards from these to make sure your dishes have sufficient time to cook.
- Correct serving times must be clearly indicated on your plan of work.

The dishes have to be served in the same order as they are eaten and at specific times, e.g.

Starter must be served 30 minutes before the end of the session.

Main course must be served 15 minutes before the end.

Dessert must be served 5 minutes before the end.

- Remember to show when you are heating or chilling your serving dishes.
- When you are testing your food for readiness, e.g. testing pasta, this must also be clearly indicated.
- Allow time to chill foods if dishes have to be served cold.
- Include putting food into the refrigerator – this shows good food hygiene.
- Check that you have included all the activities in the recipe. You don't have to write out exact details of your recipe. For example, you may want to include 'Whisk cream, cover, refrigerate' and also refer to the steps of the recipe (nos 3–4 on method) instead of writing out each detailed step from the recipe.

Top Tip
If you wish you may draw the cuts of vegetable to remind you.

- Include the cut of vegetable, e.g. dice, slice, jardinière – this will remind you to do it correctly.
- Tasting the dish and checking for seasoning should be included.
- Time for garnishing after plating before serving should be stated.
- State the times for washing dishes and tidying – clean as you go will earn you more marks!

Service details

In this section you must describe how you plan to serve your dishes. Labelled diagrams can be used and are very helpful. You will be awarded up to 7 marks for this area.

You must include the following:

- Number of plates
- Colour of plate
- Shape of plate
- Temperature of service plate/dish
- Full description of garnish/decoration

Equipment list

You have to complete an equipment list. This is not awarded any marks but is useful as a reminder of the equipment you may need to collect.

Additional food order

This is not marked but you must make sure you order any extra items, e.g. cream, garnishes and decorations.

Preparing, cooking and serving food

Your teacher will be observing you as you work so it is important you do your best. You will gain marks for everything you do correctly.

Top Tip
You must complete and serve both dishes within the 2½ hours. Dishes served after this time will not be awarded any of the marks available for the final dishes. Dishes served either more than five minutes early or late will not be awarded any marks for presentation.

How to do well in your practical assignment

Awarding of marks

Marks are awarded under three main areas.

Area 1. Working methods

This includes

1. Basic preparation skills and techniques

This will include marks awarded for

– accurate weighing and measuring of ingredients for all three courses – remember to re-weigh your prepared fruit and vegetables.

2. Flow of the work plan

– You should follow your plan of work as you have written it.
– Try to stick to your timings as accurately as possible.
– If you fall behind, do not panic! Keep working steadily and you will catch up.

3. Control of cookery processes

You must show that you are controlling and monitoring the cookery processes involved in the production of the three dishes. The processes will depend on the recipe but could include:

– simmering of a soup or sauce
– frying vegetables without colouring them
– grilling of chicken correctly
– control of oven temperature when baking a sponge.

Area 2. Dishes produced

The marks awarded will depend on the skills covered by the recipe but could include:

1. Preparation of ingredients

For example

– preparation of a roux sauce – cooking the roux, warming the milk, gradual addition of milk
– preparation of a filling – dicing onion, macedoine of vegetables
– whisking of a sponge mixture.

2. Cooking of dish/soup

For example

– frying of ingredients correctly
– rice drained after cooking
– adding ingredients at the correct stage of the recipe
– accurate timing of stages of the recipe
– assembling a dish, e.g. a gateau
– tasting of dish.

Top Tip
The garnish or decoration should not be overpowering. A minimum of two components should be used, e.g. a fruit coulis and fresh fruit decoration.

3. Finished result

For example

– serving on a clean dish which is the correct temperature – hot, warm, room temperature or cold. If you spill, wipe the serving plate immediately before placing on the serving area.
– neat, attractive appearance of dish
– correct texture, e.g. of pastry, sponge, rice
– appropriate garnish or decoration. The garnish or decoration should not be overpowering.
– taste – well flavoured, lacking in flavour.

Area 3. Professional practice

1. Observation of safety

For example

– handling sharp knives or equipment safely
– using a damp cloth or paper towel under the chopping board so that the board does not move when chopping
– assembling, using and washing electrical equipment
– correct, safe oven procedure
– safe use of hobs, e.g. turn off when finished
– use of oven gloves.

2. Observation of hygiene (personal and kitchen)

For example

– remove all jewellery before starting the assignment – earrings, rings, watches
– wear clean, protective clothing
– hair tied back or covered
– wash hands before starting the practical assignment and especially after handling high-risk foods
– nail polish removed
– avoid touching hair or skin during practical work
– cuts covered
– no coughing or sneezing over food
– tasting food with a clean teaspoon
– perishable food should be covered and stored in a refrigerator
– separate chopping boards must be used for raw and cooked products
– a 'clean as you go' approach to your work – do not allow a large build-up of dishes.

Top Tip
You are allowed to take your recipe home to practise. You could also practise other dishes with similar skills.

Assessment practice answers

Answers to Practical Skills for the Hospitality Industry (page 35)

1. A – 3 B – 1 C – 5 D – 2 E – 4

2. a. Assemble

   b. Refresh/immerse the food in iced or cold water

   c. Push it through a fine mesh sieve into a clean pan and reheat it, whisking or stirring continuously with a wooden spoon.

   d. Wash the carrot, peel and rewash.

   Cut it into pieces about 7.5 cm long.

   Cut off curved sides of carrot so it has straight sides.

   Lay it flat and cut it lengthways into slices of the required thickness.

   Arrange the strips into a row and cut across the strips into dice.

   e. Whisked sponges and meringues

   f. To get rid of cracks in the biscuit dough

   g. tender, flavour, moist

   h. Breadcrumbs

   i. Vegetable peeler, vegetable knife, cook's knife, filleting knife

   j. Chopped parsley or a swirl of cream, etc.
   Chopped parsley, parsley en branche, sliced tomato, lemon twist or butterfly, etc.
   Strawberry fan, fruit coulis, rosettes of cream, mint sprigs, etc.

Food Preparation for Healthy Eating (page 56)

1. a. Change the plain flour to half wholemeal and half plain.

   Change the margarine to polyunsaturated margarine.

   Change the bacon to back bacon or reduce quantity.

   Change milk to semi-skimmed milk.

   Change cheese to a stronger flavoured variety and reduce the quantity.

   Remove the salt as the stronger cheese will give flavour.

b. Plan of work

Times	Sequence of work	Notes
10.00–10.05 am	Personal hygiene, collect all the ingredients for pastry. Put on oven gas mark 6, 200 °C.	
10.05–10.15 am	Make pastry. Line flan ring. Leave to relax.	Relax to approx 10.20 am
10.15–10.20 am	Wash dishes. Trim pastry. Place in oven.	Ready at 10.30 am
10.20–10.30 am	Collect and prepare ingredients for filling.	
10.30–10.35 am	Check for readiness and remove pastry flan. Add ingredients to pastry flan and return quiche to oven.	Ready approx 10.50 am
10.35–10.50 am	Wash up dishes, clean unit. Wash and chop parsley. Warm serving dish and check flan for readiness.	
10.50–10.55 am	Serve quiche and complete final tidying up. Finish 10.55 am.	

2. 300 g lean minced beef – £2.34, 150 g onion – 11p, 75 g tomato ketchup – 24p, 200 g green pepper – 39p, 300 ml chopped tomatoes – 26p, 100 g kidney beans – 8p, 150 g brown rice – 23p Total cost – £3.65. Per portion – £0.91

3. a. Wet methods – boiling, stewing, pot roasting, poaching, braising and steaming
   b. Dry methods – baking, grilling, roasting, stir frying and microwaving

4. Grilling, as the fat in food melts and drips out so grilling is a healthy method of cooking and no additional fat is required.

5. Visible fat from the meat and poultry can be trimmed off before cooking and no additional fat is added. The reduction in fat lowers the risk of overweight, heart disease. Valuable nutrients will not be lost as the food and the liquid from the stew are served together; retains the nutritional value, e.g. vitamin C in vegetables which will contribute to general good health. A complete meal can be made in one container using a wide range of nutritious foods such as vegetables. Vegetables will add vitamin C and fibre to the dish. Fibre prevents constipation and bowel disorders.

6. They will increase the protein and fibre content of the dish – protein is required for normal growth and repair and fibre prevents constipation.

7. The cooking time is quick and a minimum amount of water is used.

8. In steaming food is cooked in the steam rising from boiling water. Suitable foods include fish and vegetables. As the food does not come into direct contact with water, fewer nutrients are lost. Vegetables can be cooked without salt, which reduces the risk of high blood pressure, heart disease and strokes. As no fat is required, this will reduce the risk of heart disease.

9. Because the fat will drip from the food during roasting and reduce the fat content.

10. Use only a small amount of oil, 'Fry Light' olive oil spray or use a non stick wok.

11. Because it contains Omega 3 which may reduce the risk of heart disease.

12. Little or no fat is added so this lowers the risk of obesity, heart disease. Food is cooked quickly so most nutrients are retained. Little water is used in cooking and so loss of nutrients is minimal. Vitamins are retained which contributes to general good health.
    Salt does not require to be added to vegetables so this lowers the risk of high blood pressure, heart disease and strokes.

Foods of the World (page 86)

1

a. They originated in tropical Asia and are commonly grown in India.

b. They should be stored in the salad drawer of the refrigerator.

c. Aubergines may be sliced and boiled, fried, or added to curries, chutneys, stuffed with meat and rice and then baked. Aubergines can have a bitter flavour and so are usually salted before use to remove the bitter juices.

d. Aubergines can grow in several shapes – they may be long, oval, or round, and they vary in colour from white to green to purple.

e. In tropical climates the eggplant is sown directly into the soil. It can grow from 40–150 cm tall and has large leaves that are 10–20 cm long and 5–10 cm wide. The stem is often spiny. The fruit are cut from the vine.

2. The exact content for this answer may vary depending on the sources used.

a. Neapolitan Pizza

History

The pizza started out as an ancient Roman breakfast. However, by the late 18th century it was common for the poor of the area around Naples to add tomato to their yeast-based flat bread and so the pizza was born. The dish gained in popularity and soon pizza became a tourist attraction for visitors to Naples.

Varieties

The 'Marinara' is the oldest and has a topping of tomato, oregano, extra virgin olive oil and usually garlic (named after the fisherman from the Bay of Naples who ate it after coming ashore).

The 'Margherita' was named after Queen Margherita of Savoy as she favoured the colours of the Italian flag on her pizza – green (basil leaves), white (mozzarella cheese) and red (tomatoes).

b. Samosas

History

Samosas are small filled pastries and have been a popular snack in India for centuries. It is thought they originated in Central Asia before the 10th century and arrived in India via the ancient trade routes.

Varieties

The vegetarian version contains flour, potato, onion, spices, green chilli. Non vegetarian samosas may contain minced meat or fish. The size and shape of a samosa, as well as the consistency of the pastry used, can vary although it is usually triangular. They are served accompanied by yoghurt, chopped onions and coriander. Samosas can also be prepared in a sweet form.

Garlic

Origin: Garlic is native to Asia but its use spread across the world more than 5000 years ago. It is mentioned in ancient Egyptian, Greek, Indian and Chinese writings.

Production: Garlic grows in a bulb that consists of a number of cloves. Each clove is protected by a layer of skin, but all are held together by additional layers of skin. Garlic is ready for harvesting when the tops turn a yellow brown colour, about a month after the seed stalks appear. The bulbs are lifted, the earth is shaken off and the leaves are tied at the top. The bulbs are then dried in the shade for 3–4 days. The leaves are then removed.

Storage: Dried bulbs are the most common. Store in an airy, dry place at room temperature. Ropes of strung garlic can be hung up.

Uses: Garlic can be eaten raw or cooked. The clove of garlic is peeled then the flesh is either chopped, grated or crushed. Garlic can be used in curries, marinades, a variety of meat dishes and chutneys.

Varieties: Many different types have been developed to suit different climates. Varieties include silverskin garlic, which is the most common type found in supermarkets due to its keeping qualities, artichoke, porcelain and purple stripe garlics.

Parsley

Origin: Parsley is by far the most frequently mentioned herb in recipes all over the world. It was mentioned by the ancient Romans in the 4th century BC and was sought for its medical uses. It is native to the Mediterranean area where it originally grew wild.

Production: It is easy to grow and should be grown in every herb garden. The colour of the leaf is bright to dark green and it has a mildly peppery taste.

Storage: It is best used fresh. It can be kept in the salad drawer of the refrigerator or may be frozen for cooking as dried is a poor substitute.

Uses: It is used in bouquet garni, added to sauces and stuffings, fried as an accompaniment to fish, or as a garnish sprinkled over finished dishes.

Varieties: Flat leafed, curly leafed; Hamburg parsley is grown for its roots and Neapolitan or Italian parsley is grown for its celery like stems.

3.

- Nail polish can contaminate food.
- Jewellery may harbour dirt and bacteria.
- Cigarette ash can contaminate food. People touching mouths and coughing cause infection.
- Food handler may contaminate food.

4. Prawn Bhuna

- Prawns should be stored in the refrigerator at 4° C.
- Raw prawns should be kept separate from cooked foods.
- Always marinate in the refrigerator and not in a warm kitchen.

Chicken Cacciatora

- Chicken should be stored in the refrigerator at 4° C.
- Raw chicken should be stored on the bottom shelf of the refrigerator.
- Raw chicken should be kept separate from cooked foods.
- Ensure chicken is thoroughly cooked and not pink.
- Serve immediately so it is piping hot.

Tiramisu

- Eggs should be stored in a cool place.
- The mascarpone cheese should be stored in the refrigerator.
- Store the tiramisu in the refrigerator until required.

Index

anchovy 78
apricots 66
arborio rice 77
assembling 13
aubergines 86

Bajra flour 63
baking 48
basil 76
bay leaves 76
biscuit dough 19
blanching 14
blending 15
boiling 46
  see also blanching
braising 47
bread 39, 44, 68, 70, 81
bread dough 19

carbohydrates, starchy 39
cardamom 62–63
cereals
  Indian cuisine 61, 63
  Italian cuisine 74, 77
chapatti 70
cheese 40, 43, 67, 80
chef de partie 6
chicken
  cacciatora 83
  tandoori 71
chocolate 34
chopping 16
  parsley 28
citrus fruit, garnishes 31
cleaning of equipment 9
cocoa powder 34
coconut 66
cold storage 10
commis chef 6
costing of ingredients 54
coulis, fruit 32
cream 33
cucumber garnish 30
cumin 62
cutting
  see also chopping; dicing
  machines 9
  vegetables 27

dairy food 40, 44
  Indian cuisine 61, 67
  Italian cuisine 74, 80
decorations see garnishes and decorations
dicing 17
dough
  kneading 19
  for pasta 77
dry methods for healthy cooking 48–49

eggs 41, 44
electrical equipment, safety and
  cleaning 9
equipment 13–26, 89
  safety and cleaning 9

fat
  food high in 42, 45
  rubbing into flour 23
fish (and fish dishes) 41, 44
  Indian cuisine 61, 64, 68, 72
  Italian cuisine 74, 78, 81
flour
  Bajra 63
  rubbing fat into 23
folding 18

food
  preparation see preparation
  presentation 1, 28–34
  storage 8, 10
fruit 38, 44
  coulis 32
  garnishing with 30, 31
  Indian cuisine 61, 66
  Italian cuisine 74
frying 45
  shallow 49
  stir 49

garnishes and decorations
  savoury dish 28–31
  sweet dish 32–34
ghee 67
green vegetables, pureéing 22
grilling 48

head chef 6
healthy eating 37–57
  cookery methods 46–49
  ingredients 37–43
herbs and spices
  garnishing with 30
  Indian cuisine 61, 62–63
  Italian cuisine 74, 75–76
hot pots and pans 9
hot storage 10
hygiene 7–8, 12, 91

icing sugar 34
Indian cuisine 60–72
Italian cuisine 73–85

jugs, measuring 11

kitchen
  hygiene 8, 91
  organisation 6
kneading 19
knives 16
  safety/cleaning 9

lamb 64
lasagne 84
lentils, red 63
liquidising 15

marinating 20
measuring 11
meat (and meat dishes) 41, 44
  Indian cuisine 61, 64, 68, 71
  Italian cuisine 74, 81, 83
microwaving 49
milk 40, 44
minestrone 82
mozzarella 80

okra 65
onions 65
orange, segmenting 24

paneer 67
Parma ham 78
parmesan 80
parsley 28
partie system 6
passing (straining) 21, 26
pasta 39, 44, 69, 77, 81, 84
pastries 68, 81
  dough 19
personal hygiene 7–8, 91
planning 50–53, 87, 88
poaching 47

pot roasting 48
potatoes 39, 44
  Indian cuisine 68
  Italian cuisine 81
poultry
  Indian cuisine 61, 71
  Italian cuisine 74, 83
prawns 64, 72
preparation of food 12, 13–26, 87, 90
  for healthy eating 44
presentation of food 12, 28–34
prosciutto de Parma 78
protein, non-dairy 41, 44
pulses 41, 44
  Indian cuisine 61, 63
  Italian cuisine 74, 77
pureéing 22

radicchio 79
raisins 66
rice 39, 44, 63, 77, 81
roasting 49
  pot 48
root vegetables, pureéing 22
rosemary 75
roti 70
rubbing in 23

safety 9, 12, 91
saffron 75
salt 42
sauces 15
  fruit 32
savoury dish garnishes 28–31
scales 11
scone dough 19
segmenting 24
shallow frying 49
skinning 25
soups 68, 81, 82
sous chef 6
spices see herbs and spices
spoons, measuring 11
spring onion curls 30
starchy carbohydrates 39
steaming 47
stewing 46
stir frying 49
storage, food 8, 10
straining (passing) 21, 26
strawberry fans 32
sugar 42, 44
  icing 34
sultanas 66
sweet dishes
  decorations 32–34
  Indian cuisine 68
  Italian cuisine 81, 85

tandoori chicken 71
time 50, 51, 52, 87
tiramisu 85
tomatoes 79
  garnishing with 29
  skinning 25
turmeric 62

vegetables 38, 44
  cutting 27
  Indian cuisine 61, 65, 68
  Italian cuisine 74, 79, 81
  pureéing 22

weighing 11

yoghurt 40, 67

Indexer: Dr Laurence Errington